ENDINGS

ENDINGS

*Death,
Glorious and Otherwise,
As Faced by Ten Outstanding
Figures of Our Time*

BY LEON PROCHNIK

CROWN PUBLISHERS, INC.   NEW YORK

Inquiries should be addressed to Crown Publishers, Inc., One Park Avenue, New York, New York 10016

Printed in the United States of America
Published simultaneously in Canada by General Publishing Company Limited

Library of Congress Cataloging in Publication Data

Prochnik, Leon.
  Endings: death, glorious and otherwise, as faced by ten outstanding figures of our time.

  1. Biography–20th century. 2. Death–Case studies. I. Title.
CT120.P76 1980   920'.009'04   79-19501
ISBN: 0-517-53405-3

DESIGNED BY SHARI DE MISKEY

10 9 8 7 6 5 4 3 2 1
First edition

Since this page cannot accommodate the permissions, they appear on page vi.

For Nicole
Who wanted to know

CONTENTS

Human life, because it is marked
by a beginning and an end, becomes
whole, an entity in itself that
can be subjected to judgement, only
when it has ended in death; death
not merely ends life, it also bestows
upon it a silent completeness, snatched
from the hazardous flux to which all
things human are subject.

—HANNAH ARENDT
The Life of the Mind

This is my death and it will profit me
to understand it.

—ANNE SEXTON

The dead don't die. They look on
and help.

—D. H. LAWRENCE
Selected Letters
of D. H. Lawrence

PREFACE

In most biographies death is relegated to the final pages. In this book it has been granted center stage. For the famous people whose ends are recounted here all died legendary deaths.

Some of these endings were violent, some lingering, some blessedly swift. But whether they were cowardly or heroic, willed, accidental, or desperately struggled against, all have since achieved the stature of myth.

In part I think this is due to their extraordinary drama, in part because the lives they terminated were themselves extraordinary, and, perhaps most importantly, because—as legends do—they illuminate basic truths about our own deaths and lives.

Perhaps that is why in the coure of writing this book I have frequently felt I was confronting my own biography. For in the endings of these ten men and women I have found my emotions mirrored to a degree far beyond anything I originally anticipated. And, to my even greater surprise, the more I have allowed myself to acknowledge the deep feelings of kinship and empathy stirred in me by their deaths, the more I have come to cherish my own aliveness.

SIGMUND FREUD

Until he was stricken with cancer at the age of sixty-seven, Sigmund Freud was an astonishingly youthful and vigorous man. At sixty-five he had climbed the Brocken, a mountain peak in Germany nearly four thousand feet high. Nearing his seventh decade he maintained an awesome schedule of study, writing, lecturing, and psychoanalyzing patients that occupied him from eight o'clock each morning until the late hours of the night. His correspondence with admirers and disciples throughout the world alone would have taxed the energies of most men half his age.

In 1917, Freud had first noticed a painful swelling in his palate. He was a compulsive smoker—twenty cigars a day—and the swelling ironically occurred as World War I cut into his supply of cigars and just as ironically subsided as soon as he resumed his heavy smoking. Freud, who until then had never been seriously ill in his life, and who believed he was fated to die of heart disease, paid no attention to this first ominous warning signal.

Then, in February 1923, the swelling recurred, this time no longer as a mere symptom. "I detected two months ago a leucoplactic growth on my jaw and palate, right side," he wrote dispassionately to a friend, "which I had removed. I was assured it was benign but as you know, nobody could guarantee its behavior were it permitted to grow further."

The operation which he alluded to so unemotionally in his letter had, in fact, nearly resulted in his death. Ineptly performed in a daytime clinic (Freud, ever one to minimize his personal problems, had wished to avoid the fuss associated with his entering a hospital), the surgery had triggered considerable bleeding and over-night accommodations had to be hastily improvised. Freud was housed in a makeshift ward with a cretinous dwarf and awoke to another attack of massive hemor-rhaging. Choking on the sudden accumulation of blood in his mouth, he could not call out, the night bell did not work, and it took his retarded roommate to sum-mon help and save the famed psychoanalyst's life.

Worse yet was the aftermath of the surgery. The surgeon had neglected to take the necessary steps to guard against shrinkage of the operational scar. The result was a permanent contraction of Freud's mouth that was to cause him untold hardship and suffering for the rest of his life. Furthermore, the "leucoplactic growth" he had been assured was benign had, in reality, turned out to be cancerous.

In September of the same year the cancer reap-peared, and a second, drastically more radical opera-tion was performed. This time Freud's lip and cheek had to be split wide open and the entire jaw and palate on the affected (right) side removed. Also excised was part of the tongue, the entire procedure carried out under local anesthetic. A week after the operation— unable to talk and fed through a nasal tube—Freud wrote to a friend:

DEAR INCORRIGIBLE OPTIMIST

Tampon removed today. Out of bed. What is left of me put into clothes. As soon as I can sleep without an injection, I shall go home.

So began sixteen years of almost continuous physical suffering. A hulking prosthesis—a form of magnified denture designed to shut off his upper mouth from his nasal cavity—caused Freud such unrelieved misery that he ruefully nicknamed it "the monster." For Freud to be able to speak and eat, the prosthesis had to be conformed snugly to his palate, its tight fit causing him constant irritation and excruciating pain. Yet the removal of the piece for more than a few hours invariably resulted in shrinkage of the surrounding tissue and necessitated major alteration of the hated denture before it could be reinserted. For Freud, who had always taken great pleasure in food, eating was now an agony, and from here on in he would rarely take his meals in the presence of others. In talking he frequently had to keep the prosthesis in place with his thumb. For the remainder of his days Freud's speech would be defective—nasal and thick, its quality similar to that produced by a cleft palate. His hearing, also impaired by the operation, would soon leave him totally deaf on his right side—his "listening" side—so that the position of his chair and his famed analyst's couch had to be reversed.

Yet with all the suffering, with thirty-one operations still ahead of him—an average of one every six months for the rest of his life—Freud's stoical philosophy of life not only allowed him to endure but to press on with his work. "I have never realized," he wrote, "that the older one grows, the more there is to do—the idea of peaceful old age seems as much of a myth as that of happy youth." In the years remaining to him Freud would both originate and develop some of his most ambitiously complex theories. In addition, through his ceaseless output of scientific papers, his continual organizing of international conferences, and his unflagging correspondence with other analysts around the world, he continued tirelessly to advance the cause of psychoanalysis.

In January 1924, four months after the radical surgery on his jaw, Freud began to see patients again. Though he was now in almost constant pain he felt the need to resume income-producing work. Medical costs from his illness were beginning to accumulate and he was determined to pay all his doctor bills in full. For a fraction of what a Park Avenue analyst would charge today, Freud earned a modest living treating six patients daily.

From the start of his illness until his death, his only unmarried daughter and closest confidante, Anna, was his sole nurse. She would change his postoperative dressings, help him insert and remove the dreaded prosthesis, and watch for any signs of renewed malignancy. With Anna he made this pact: all treatment must be performed in a totally matter-of-fact fashion. Regardless of how dire his condition, there were to be no sentiment, no pity, no scenes—Anna was to attend to him with the cool, objective detachment of a surgeon.

Pressing on with his work as psychoanalyst and author, Freud gained ever-greater fame and renown even as he continued to struggle against the ravages of his illness. Widely honored on his seventy-fifth birthday, he commented: "How preferable to all this a bearable prosthesis would be—one that didn't clamor to be the main object of one's existence."

Yet for all his suffering, he found that he could not abandon his smoking. Attempts to renounce what he called the "sweet habit" invariably resulted in a marked diminution of his intellectual interests. "Abstinence is not justified at my age," he maintained, though to get a cigar into his mouth now required him to force his bite open with the help of a clothespin.

In 1926, in addition to his jaw-eroding cancer, Freud developed heart trouble (angina pectoris) and recuperated briefly at a sanatorium where he nonetheless continued to treat his own patients. Upon returning to Vienna he allowed himself to be taken for morning drives and for the first time he discovered something his work-filled days had deprived him of until then—the beauty of lilac-filled Vienna in early spring. "What a pity," he wrote, "that one has to grow old and ill before making this discovery."

In 1929, after six years of operations, X-ray treatments, and endless refittings of his prosthesis (by then a special treatment room had been set up for him in his own house), a friend of Freud's persuaded him to engage a doctor who could watch over his health on a day-to-day basis. The doctor was Max Schur, a young internist of excellent reputation who had the additional advantage of having received analytic training. From their first meeting, the young doctor and the aging founder of psychoanalysis took to each other. Freud told Schur that he must never keep the truth from him, no matter how harsh that truth might be. "I can stand a great deal of pain and I hate sedatives," he confided to Schur. Then, fixing Schur with his dark, penetrating eyes, he added meaningfully, "I trust you will not let me suffer unnecessarily."

From that time on Schur and Freud's devoted daughter, Anna, jointly maintained daily watch over their patient, doing everything in their power to see to his comfort, constantly on the alert for the slightest sign of change in his condition. Freud, who was capable of Jehovah-like outbursts of anger in defense of his work, was, and would remain to the end, a model patient, grateful, cooperative, and uncomplaining, no matter how pronounced his distress. In the face of his fearful illness he remained unshakably stoical, maintaining to the end that there was no use "quarreling with fate," focusing, as best he could, on life's benedictions. "Do not make the mistake of thinking I am depressed," he wrote to a doctor friend. "I regard it as a triumph to retain a clear judgment in all circumstances. . . . To grow so old; to find so much warm love in family and

friends; so much expectation of success in such a
venturesome undertaking [psychoanalysis] . . . who else
has attained so much?"

During the next seven years, as Freud and his work
received ever-greater recognition throughout the
world, his physical suffering grew progressively more
intense. Typically, in the spring of 1929 there was a trip
to Berlin for the fitting of a new prosthesis. In October
of the same year, an operation to excise part of a scar
that had been previously burned. In February of 1930,
another operation. In April, yet another. In August,
still one more in the endless series of attempts to
remodel the prosthesis. Five operations in all before the
year was out.

In July 1936, after thirteen years of these "preven-
tive" operations, unmistakable cancer was once again
found to be present in Freud's mouth. No longer would
Freud's doctors be able to ward off the disease by
removing precancerous tissue. From now on there
would be a constant recurrence of the malignancy. The
smallest suspicious spots now had to be burned away
with ever-increasing frequency, further impairing
Freud's ability to eat and drink. During one of these
procedures the normally imperturbable Freud unnerved his doctors by suddenly crying out, "I can't go
on any longer!"

Nonetheless, he endured Prometheus-like, continuing to write, to see patients, and refusing all drugs.
"I prefer to think in torment," he maintained, "than not
to be able to think clearly."

In May 1938, in addition to his monumental physical
suffering, the takeover of Austria by the Nazis forced
Freud, who was Jewish, to flee his beloved Vienna with
his family and seek refuge in England. He had hardly
settled into his new home in London when yet another

jaw operation was deemed necessary by his doctors. In accordance with their decision to slit open his cheek to gain better access to the problem area, Freud's famous beard—by now the virtual trademark of psycho-analysis—had to be shaved. The operation, the most radical since the original surgery in 1923, left Freud utterly spent. He never fully recovered from its effects.

At Christmastime a swelling appeared in his right cheek—one that took on an increasingly ominous ap-pearance with the passing weeks. In February 1939 a biopsy disclosed an unmistakable malignancy, but this time the surgeons could do no more. The tumor was inaccessible. The case was now listed as "inoperable, incurable cancer." From then on, the only treatment would be X rays to slow the spread of the disease.

In April, in a letter to one of his close associates, Freud wrote:

> The people around me have tried to wrap me in a cocoon of optimism: the cancer is shrink-ing, the reactions to the treatment are only temporary, etc. I don't believe any of it and don't like being deceived.

In June, in another letter to the same associate:

> The radium has once more begun to eat in, with pain and toxic effects, and my world is again what it was before—a little island of pain floating on a sea of indifference.

And to another long-time friend he wrote:

> There is no doubt that I have a new recur-rence of my dear old cancer with which I have

been sharing my existence for sixteen years.
Which of us would prove to be the stronger
we could not at that time predict.

By July 1939, Freud had lost an alarming amount of
weight and had begun to grow apathetic. A cancerous
ulceration was now visible on his cheek and his daughter Anna was forced to minister to him day and night.
For the first time since the beginning of his illness,
Freud permitted himself to take drugs—an occasional
dose of aspirin. Even more amazingly, he continued to
press on with both his writing and his analytical work,
seeing four patients a day till the end of July.

Throughout August, Freud's condition rapidly deteriorated. His remarkable ability to sleep even at the
worst of times now deserted him. A rancid odor began
to emanate from his ulcerated cheek, the smell of it so
offensive that his pet dog shied away from him. No
longer strong enough to work, Freud spent his days in a
sick bay in his study gazing out at the flowers of his
English garden. It was a paradoxical summer—the
most beautiful one in decades, the sun shining bril-
liantly day after day while World War II drew ever
nearer. To the end Freud insisted on remaining fully
informed about what was going on in the world, closely
following international events in the daily newspapers.
When one of his physicians inquired if he thought the
coming war would be the last, Freud replied, "It is *my*
last war, anyhow." Of the last book he read—a novel by
Balzac—he commented: "The perfect book for me. It
deals with starvation." Unable to eat, totally devoid of
appetite, he himself was little more than a skeleton by
now.

In the weeks that followed, the cancer inexorably ate
its way through his cheek, the accompanying pain
growing more agonizing by the day. Finally, on Septem-

ber 21, Freud could bear it no longer. To his devoted personal physician, Dr. Schur, he said: "My dear Schur, you remember our first talk. You promised me you would assist me when I could no longer carry on. It is strictly torture now. It no longer makes any sense." Then, after a moment's hesitation, he added quietly: "Tell Anna about our talk."

The following morning, having informed Anna of his conversation with her father, Dr. Schur complied with Freud's wish and injected his famous patient with a third of a grain of morphine. Given Freud's weakened condition and his all but total abstinence from drugs during his illness, the dose was sufficient. Freud uttered a sigh of relief and sank into a deep sleep from which he never awakened. He died shortly before midnight of the following day—September 23, 1939. He was eighty-three years old.

On September 26, at a ceremony in Golders Green, London, attended by some of the world's greatest scientists and artists, Sigmund Freud's body was cremated.

To this day his ashes repose there in a Grecian urn he was especially fond of.

HARRY HOUDINI

EXCEPT FOR HIS HEIGHT OF FIVE AND A HALF FEET, everything about Harry Houdini seemed larger than life. He billed himself as The Handcuff King, The Escapist Extraordinary, The Master Monarch of Modern Mystery, The Supreme Ruler of Magic, The Greatest Mystifier That History Chronicles. And, astonishingly, these and the dozens of equally grandiose-sounding titles that were bestowed upon him throughout his career were not exaggerations. From the moment the curtain rose on a Houdini performance and, attired in evening clothes, he stepped briskly up to the footlights with a "Good evening, ladies and gentlemen, let us begin," audiences were gripped by his messianic air of authority. With his piercing blue-gray eyes and classically chiseled features exuding the moral dignity of an ancient Roman consul, his German-accented voice reaching the farthest stall with magisterial self-confidence, Houdini had his viewers under his spell long before the actual show had begun.

And what shows he gave! At his command, dancing girls materialized out of nowhere and full-grown elephants vanished into air; he chopped beautiful assistants into pieces and reassembled them at will; he whipped endless silk streamers from empty glass bowls and walked through walls of solid brick. But though Houdini was a brilliant illusionist and consummate magician, though his stage presence was such that he could hold audiences for hours on end with sheer talk, his most amazing feats, the true source of his enormous popularity, were his "escapes." For thirty years he invited countless challengers to strap, shackle, manacle, and otherwise bind him with an unending array of restraining devices. He arranged to have himself immersed upside-down in water-filled cans, sewn into canvas seabags, bound in straightjackets, locked into steel safes. He let himself be confined naked inside an "escape-proof" prison van, chained to the arm of a whirling windmill, dropped to the bottom of the Mississippi in a sealed strongbox, lashed to the mouth of a cannon whose fuse was lit—and each time, overcoming seemingly impossible obstacles, mobilizing skill and willpower to produce results that seemed truly miraculous, he fought his way to freedom.

Because his greatest feats invariably represented a triumph over death, Houdini early on became the object of fervent hero worship, many of his admirers being convinced that he possessed supernatural powers. Though Houdini publicly denied this, insisting that his "magic" was essentially nothing more than skill and hard work, he had, from the very start of his career, encouraged audiences to believe in his invincibility, and, as his fame grew, he came to believe in it more and more himself. It was this conviction that gave him the confidence to devise stunts no others would dare to attempt (at one point in his career he seriously contemplated attempting to free himself while hurtling over Niagara Falls in a barrel), that sustained him through countless brushes with death, and that finally, ironically, proved the undoing of the man the world had come to regard as a seemingly indestructible life-force.

He had been born Ehrich Weiss on July 22, 1874, in Appleton, Wisconsin, the fifth child of an impoverished immigrant rabbi and a wife twenty-five years his junior, and grew up in extreme poverty ("We lived there, I mean *starved* there," he wrote years later of the New York East Side flat in which the Weiss clan resided). While still a child he was exhorted by his father to prepare himself to be the family's mainstay. At the age of twelve he ran away from home and for a year sought his fortune following traveling shows and circuses. At fourteen he learned his first coin trick and decided to make magic his life's work. At sixteen he discovered the memoirs of France's greatest magician, Robert-Houdin, audaciously added an *i* to his hero's name and became Houdini (where "Harry" came from, no one knows for certain to this day).

From the start he possessed the ideal ingredients for transforming himself into the "Undisputed Master of Escape"—a superbly conditioned athlete's body, a cool head, and a nearly superhuman ability to withstand discomfort and pain. Equally, if not more important, was his passion for testing himself beyond the limits of ordinary endurance, his fierce determination to prove to himself and the world that there was no challenge— the more dangerous the better—over which he could not triumph.

To facilitate his hair-raising feats of self-liberation, he developed total physical self-control—he taught himself to untie knots with his toes, to expand and contract virtually every part of his body at will, to swallow and disgorge items the size of a handball (a foolproof method of secreting escape tools). To prepare for the leaps he planned to make handcuffed and chained into freezing rivers, he trained nightly at home, submerging himself for ever-increasing periods of time in a bathtub filled with ice. For weeks on end he practiced extricating himself from straightjackets while hanging upside-down, mastered the art, and gave America's cities a new spectator sport—the Great Houdini squirming free as he dangled fearlessly from their highest skyscrapers.

He was twenty, and still a half dozen years away from fame, when he met his wife-to-be, a petite eighteen-year-old singer-dancer from Brooklyn by the name of

Wilhelmina Beatrice Rahner. Houdini's courting of her was a characteristically whirlwind affair. Bess was in the front row, when in the midst of his performance Houdini knocked over a glass of colored liquid, spotting her dress. To make amends, he got her to give him her measurements, talked his mother into making her a new dress, personally delivered it to Bess's house, whisked her off to Coney Island, and there proposed to her. Before the evening was over, they were married.

From then until the end of his life, Bess and he were inseparable. She traveled with him, was frequently part of his act, and devotedly monitored his "escapes" from backstage (whenever they took too long, she would go into hysterics or faint). He, for his part, whether he was away or at home, wrote his wife a love letter every day for the next thirty years.

Equally fervent was Houdini's devotion to his mother. Having sworn at his father's deathbed that he would look after her, he provided for his mother's comfort and well-being on a scale that went beyond her wildest expectations. He moved her into a fine large brownstone on upper Broadway. On a visit to London he bought her a dress that had been designed for Queen Victoria and persuaded her to wear it at a family reunion. On another occasion he had his salary paid to him in gold coins so he could shower them into her outstretched apron.

He was thirty-nine years old and on one of his numerous European tours when news of her death reached him. He fell unconscious to the floor of his dressing room. He insisted on seeing her before she was buried, would not accept that she was dead until he had personally pressed his ear to her heart (could the mother of the greatest death-defier the world had ever known be mortal?).

Unable to accept the finality of his mother's death,

desperate to make contact with her at any price, Houdini began attending seances. It was a situation both poignant and ironic: the world's greatest master of deception hoping against hope that what he knew to be a fraud (as a young magician he had briefly tried his hand at spiritualism) would somehow, in this single instance, prove to be genuine.

But though he fervently wanted to believe ("I waited, hoping I might feel once more the presence of my beloved Mother," he wrote after one of countless attempts to establish contact), the seances he attended, with their shabby illusions and obvious trickery, appalled him. At one such sitting, presided over by the wife of Sir Arthur Conan Doyle, the creator of Sherlock Holmes, Houdini's mother purportedly sent him a lengthy message in perfect English, a language she could neither speak nor write while alive. When at last he could no longer suspend his disbelief and was forced to admit it was all a sickening sham, he turned on spiritualism and its practitioners with an anger born of bitter disillusionment.

At the pinnacle of his career, with offers of ten times more bookings than he could possibly fulfill, he now began to devote more and more of his time to the exposure of fake supernatural phenomena. Subjecting spiritualism and its practitioners to the same investigative scrutiny he had once lavished on the mechanisms of locks, he challenged any medium to demonstrate powers that he could not expose or reproduce. When *Scientific American* offered a twenty-five-hundred-dollar reward "for the first physical manifestation of a psychic nature produced under scientific control," Houdini persuaded the magazine to create an investigating committee, had himself appointed to its board, and exposed each and every applicant for the prize.

Over the next decade he crisscrossed the country

lecturing tirelessly on the subject, amassed the world's largest private library of occult literature, wrote a best-selling exposé about mediums—*A Magician Among the Spirits*—testified on their practices before a committee of Congress, and, finally, in 1925, took to the road with the most ambitious show of his career—one that combined the exposure of spiritualistic phenomena with an elaborate magic revue and the greatest of his death-defying escapes.

Houdini, who was now fifty-two years old, had of late been showing the first signs of exhaustion. Early in the tour he contracted a cold, a rarity for him. Previously able to get by on five hours' sleep a night, he now slept with a black bandage over his eyes and a small pillow under his side to ease an old kidney injury incurred during an escape fourteen years earlier.

Nonetheless, he continued to push himself, as he always had, to the very limits of his endurance. He exercised rigorously every day; to climax his show's second act he chose the Chinese Water Torture Cell number, an especially arduous escape in which he was deposited head-first into a chained cage that sat immersed inside a water-filled tank; when he wasn't performing, his dawn-to-dusk work schedule included looking after the business end of the show (he was its producer and director as well as its star), devising new publicity stunts, answering an ever-increasing flood of fan mail, and writing a daily newspaper column. Even though the tour was the most strenuously demanding one he had ever undertaken, he continued to accept speaking engagements whenever and wherever he could.

In October 1926, while the show was playing at the Providence Opera House, Bess suddenly took ill. Houdini, who only consulted doctors on his own behalf when forced to by Bess, hastily summoned one for his wife and was told that she was suffering from ptomaine poisoning. He sat up with Bess for two nights, then, her fever having abated, traveled to New York by train for an urgent conference with his lawyer (an army of irate spiritualists were suing him for a total of more than a million dollars).

He caught up with Bess and the show in Albany the following day, having spent a third sleepless night on the train. Though he only had time for a brief nap before that evening's performance, as he stepped up to the footlights smiling, he appeared as bright and alert as ever.

During the second act, however, the months of accumulating fatigue finally took their toll. As Houdini, clad in a bathing suit, was being hoisted into the air upside-down in preparation for the Chinese Water Torture Cell escape, the metal frame that held his legs suddenly jerked, the abruptness of the movement catching the exhausted magician unprepared. Signaling his assistants to lower him back down to the ground, Houdini attempted to stand and found that he couldn't. A doctor, hurriedly called up to the stage, probed his left ankle and announced it was fractured. Houdini, promising he would have it attended to immediately after the show, changed back into his evening clothes and, to the delight of the audience, continued with his performance, capping it with a lively, hour-long exposé of mediums and their practices.

Though the next day's newspapers predicted that the accident was likely to keep him off the stage for weeks or even months to come, Houdini fashioned a special brace for his ankle, finished his remaining two days in Albany, took the show to Schenectady for its scheduled three days there, and a week later opened at the Princess Theatre in Montreal.

The following day, in a characteristic flurry of activity, he oversaw preparations for that evening's performance, addressed members of Montreal's Police Department, then rushed over to McGill University, where, fulfilling a long-standing commitment to speak, he delivered a lecture on spiritualism to a large assembly of faculty and students.

At the end of the lecture, he sat in a chair on the speakers' platform, shaking hands with the numerous members of the audience who thronged up to see him. One young admirer, Samuel J. Smiley, showed Houdini a sketch he had made of him while he had been delivering his talk. Houdini complimented him on the likeness, autographed the drawing, and invited Smiley to come backstage later in the week to do a close-up portrait.

Four days later, on October 22, still hobbled by the injury to his ankle, he met Smiley and a fellow student named Jack Price in the lobby of the Princess Theatre at eleven in the morning and the three proceeded to the magician's dressing room for the promised portrait session. Once inside the room, Houdini took off his coat and jacket and settled himself on a couch. As Smiley began to work on his portrait, Houdini busied himself going through a pile of mail that had accumulated on his dressing-room table.

A short while later they were joined by a third McGill student, a nervously intense young man with thinning red hair who was returning a book of magic he had borrowed from Houdini. The name of the visitor was J. Gordon Whitehead. He was over six feet tall, powerfully built, and a member of the school's boxing team. Houdini introduced him to his other two guests and went on sorting his mail.

In an attempt to make conversation, Whitehead tried to engage Houdini in a discussion of biblical miracles.

Houdini did not appear especially interested in the subject. Pressed by Whitehead, Houdini briefly speculated about what people of antiquity would have made of his kind of magic, then busied himself again with his letters.

A few moments later, as Houdini rose to prepare for his matinee performance, Whitehead asked him if it was true that he could withstand heavy punches to his midsection. Houdini appeared amused by the question; though he had alluded to this test during his McGill lecture, inviting members of the audience to challenge his prowess in this fashion had been one of his earliest routines, discarded long ago for feats infinitely more sophisticated and daring. When Whitehead, persisting, asked if he could attempt a few trial punches, Houdini, still absorbed in reading through his mail, nodded his assent. The overzealous Whitehead, thinking this a signal to proceed with the test, struck his unprepared host full-force in the abdomen three times in rapid succession. Horrified, Smiley and Price jumped forward to intercede, but it was Houdini, his face momentarily contorted with pain, who, quickly recovering, signaled Whitehead to stop. Explaining that it was essential that he be allowed to brace himself properly before a punch was thrown, Houdini, ever the showman, invited the student to try once again. The contrite Whitehead hesitated. When at last he complied, his fist bounced off Houdini's midsection without any effect; the magician's abdominal muscles, when contracted, were as hard as oak.

But the initial blows had done irreparable damage. By the end of his matinee performance, Houdini was conscious of a rapidly growing soreness in his stomach. By late afternoon his entire abdominal area was unbearably tender to the touch and he experienced an agonizingly burning sensation with every step he took.

Any other man would have doubled over, called out for help, and very likely been saved. Houdini, with his aversion to doctors, with his unshakable faith in his indestructibility, with a lifetime of mind and body control to aid him, fought back the pain and stubbornly, dangerously, went on to perform again that very same evening. By all accounts he gave an exceptionally brilliant performance.

By the time he got to bed that night, however, the pain was so intense that he could not sleep. He told Bess that it was nothing more serious than a cramp or a pulled muscle. A concerned Bess insisted on massaging his stomach. When she was done, Houdini thanked her, assuring her that her magic touch had cured him. As soon as she had fallen asleep, he resumed writhing in agony.

In the morning he got himself out of the house before Bess awoke, leaving behind a typically cheerful note. "Champagne Coquette," it read (the night before, masking his injury, he had arranged an impromptu champagne party for his recuperating wife and her nurse), "I'll be at the theatre at 12:00 P.M." The doting husband who frequently identified himself as "Houdinsky" and "Who-dee-knee" in the playful daily missives he sent her, this morning had signed off, almost apologetically, as "H. H. Fall Guy."

But although the note attempted to be amusing, Houdini's struggle against the growing torment caused by his injury was deadly grim. During a day most of which he spent locked in his dressing room fighting back ever-increasing pain, Houdini, incredibly, willed his way through a matinee and evening performance, then left by train with Bess for Detroit (he was scheduled to open at the Garrick Theatre there the following evening for a two-week run). But by now the searing pain in his stomach was too great even for him to disguise. Bess's nurse took his temperature. It was 102 degrees. (Bess, hardly recovered from her bout with ptomaine poisoning, collapsed when she learned of the blows to the stomach her husband had received.) At Bess's frantic insistence an urgent telegram was sent ahead to Detroit requesting that the best doctor in town be waiting to give Houdini a thorough examination the moment they arrived at their hotel.

The train, however, was late reaching Detroit and there was a mad rush to get props and equipment to the theater in time for the show. Houdini, frantic to distract himself from his pain, insisted on going directly to the theater with the rest of the company. Once there, he busied himself helping to set up the heavy, elaborate apparatus for that night's performance.

Shortly before curtain time a doctor finally arrived at the Garrick Theatre. His name was Leo Dretzka; he had been waiting for Houdini at his hotel for hours, was on his way to an important out-of-town medical convention, and already had missed several trains. He examined a stripped Houdini on the floor of the star's dressing room (there was neither a couch nor a cot in the room for Houdini to lie on). He told the magician that he was suffering from acute appendicitis and that an ambulance must be called immediately. Houdini, informed by the manager of the theater that the house was sold out, assured Dr. Dretzka he would go to a hospital the moment the show was over. Dr. Dretzka insisted he must go now. Houdini was equally adamant in refusing. The doctor, in a hurry to catch his train, regretfully departed. Houdini, aware that tonight would be his last performance, somehow managed to get himself into his evening clothes.

It was a captivating show that he gave that night, with

only his assistants aware of the life-and-death drama that was unfolding. To the audience out front, the dynamic figure that marched on stage to the strains of "Pomp and Circumstance" was the Houdini of old. For a full hour he held the packed house with his dazzling array of tricks. Then, as the curtain closed, he collapsed. He was carried to his dressing room. His temperature was now 104.

Even so, he insisted on completing the show. Propped up in a chair for the second act, he gave his standard lecture-demonstration on spiritualism, then patiently answered questions from the audience. Though his voice occasionally trailed off in midsentence, though his face was a grinning mask of perspiration, Houdini's self-control was such that not a single person in the theater suspected they were watching a mortally ill man. It was only when he had taken his final bows, when the curtain had closed for the last time, that he collapsed again.

Still he refused to go to a hospital. Instead, mobilizing a final reserve of willpower, he changed his clothes and went to his hotel. There, a hysterical Bess summoned the hotel physician. It was three o'clock in the morning when Dr. Charles S. Kennedy, a noted Detroit surgeon sent for by the hotel's doctor, arrived at the Houdinis' suite. The briefest of examinations was enough for Kennedy to announce that Houdini must be rushed to the hospital at once. Even then the magician resisted. Only after he had put through a long-distance call to his personal physician in New York and been begged by him to comply, only when he was once more on the brink of unconsciousness—the pain unendurable now, even for him—did Houdini finally allow an ambulance to be called.

He was sped from his hotel to Grace Hospital where

in the early hours of Monday, October 25, his ruptured appendix, horribly gangrenous, was at last removed. The doctors who performed the operation marveled that Houdini was still alive. Peritonitis was far advanced. During the four days he had stubbornly resisted help, enormous quantities of poison had circulated throughout his sytem. There was agreement among the doctors that they could have easily saved him had he been operated on in time. Now there was little more they could do than ease his pain. The prognosis was grim: extensive infection of the peritoneal cavity was in those days irreversible. He might live another twelve hours, certainly no more than twenty-four.

To their astonishment, Houdini hung on. Bess, who had suffered a relapse, was assigned a room in the same hospital and paid him daily visits. His sister and two of his brothers arrived hurriedly from New York to be at his bedside. Medical bulletins on his condition were bannered on the front pages of newspapers around the world. Wishes for his recovery poured in.

Struggling to survive, Houdini made it through Tuesday, Wednesday, Thursday. His spirits rose. He jokingly told his brothers and sister their long trip had been unnecessary. He reassured Bess he would be up and about in no time. He chatted with his doctors and nurses. Another magical Houdini escape seemed in the offing.

Then, on Friday, October 29, Houdini suffered a sudden relapse; acute streptococcus peritonitis had set in. A second operation was hurriedly performed. And still, to the wonder of his doctors, Houdini continued to do battle. Haggard, black circles under his eyes, drains protruding from his abdomen, even now the tenacious miracle-worker would not accept that he was dying.

One of the last things he whispered to Bess was to remember the words *"Rosabelle—Believe."* "Rosabelle" was the first song he had ever heard her sing; *believe* was a code word Bess and he had frequently used when performing mind-reading tricks together. The man who for more than a decade had waged unremitting war against spiritualism was with his final breaths offering his wife a password with which he would try to reach her from beyond the grave.

By Saturday the guarded bulletins put out by the hospital described his condition as "less than favorable." Finally, on Sunday morning, The World Famous Self-Liberator, who for close to four decades had thrilled countless thousands with his displays of courage and will, could struggle no longer.

"I'm tired of fighting," he whispered to his brother. "I guess this is going to get me." Having said this, Houdini closed his eyes and lay still. When he briefly opened them for the last time, Bess was leaning over him, crying. Though Houdini tried, he could no longer speak. Bess put her arms around him. Houdini looked at her for a long moment. Then his head fell back on his pillow.

The great magician, whose life had been an un-broken series of triumphs over seemingly insurmountable challenges, died in a coma at 1:26 P.M. the same afternoon, October 31, 1926. His body was returned to New York in a bronze coffin that had accompanied him on the tour—a coffin in which he had intended to attempt to set a new world record for remaining buried alive the longest period of time.

After an emotional ceremony attended by more than two thousand people, he was laid to rest in the family plot at the Machpelah Cemetery in Brooklyn, a black bag containing his mother's letters nestled under his head.

Among his personal effects, Bess, who for the rest of her life would wait in vain for her husband's message from beyond the grave, found the last letter he had written to her a few days before his death:

SWEETHEART—

When you read this I shall be dead. Dear Heart, do not grieve. I shall be at rest by the side of my beloved parents, and wait for you . . .

> Yours in Life, Death
> and Ever After,
>
> HOUDINI

ROBERT FALCON SCOTT

As heroic statues go, the bronze figure of Commander Scott that stands in Waterloo Place, London, is relatively modest. Sculpted by his wife, it shows the famed explorer in polar garb staring intently into the distance. Vision, determination, fortitude, courage—the resolute, finely chiseled face suggests all these inspiring traits without forcing them upon the viewer. What it does not show—what its subject himself attempted to conceal until the very end—is the tortured persona behind the confident facade; the brooding, driven, self-doubting man whose need to prove himself forced him to pursue a quest that ended in failure and death, and in doing so ironically won him the recognition and acclaim that in life had always eluded him.

Robert Falcon Scott—"Con" to his family and friends—was born in Devon, England, on June 6, 1868. A brewer's son, the third of five children, he was a shy, retiring child, pampered by his three sisters and deeply attached to his mother, a strong-willed, demanding woman who from the first instilled in him a strict sense of obedience and duty. In 1881, at the age of thirteen, he was enrolled in the navy, and two years later assigned to his first seagoing ship. It was a harshly rigorous life that soon toughened him physically. But although Scott rapidly acquired the trappings of the ideal young officer—unflappable efficiency, an appetite for hard work, a talent for commanding others— inwardly he never got over the shock of having been wrenched away from his family and, what was worse, compounded his suffering by blaming himself for failing to make the adjustment ("How can I bear it," he lamented in a secret diary, chastising himself for his feelings of homesickness, uncertainty, and fear. "I write of the future; of the hopes of being more worthy; but shall I ever be?").

By the time Scott was twenty he had served on a half dozen ships, and, graduating first in his class, was promoted to lieutenant. Even for a gifted young officer, however, advancement in the British navy of that day was agonizingly slow. He was twenty-nine and still drawing a lieutenant's meager pay when within a year the sudden deaths of first his father and then his brother threw the full support of his family on his shoulders. A period of extreme financial hardship followed that was to leave Scott fearful of failure and poverty for the rest of his life. Already frugal, he now denied himself even the most basic needs, passing up shore leaves, paring his mess bills to the bone, struggling to make do with frayed uniforms in a service where smartness of dress was essential to any hope of success. And then, in his thirtieth year, when his prospects seemed dimmest, a chance meeting with an enterprising geographer dramatically altered the course of his life.

A dozen years earlier, as an eighteen-year-old midshipman, Scott had made a lasting impression on Clements Markham, the man who was soon to become president of England's Royal Geographical Society. After watching the fledgling young officer lead his crew of sailors to victory in a hotly contested sailboat race, Markham had asked to meet Scott, had been greatly impressed by his intelligence, seriousness, and manly bearing, and had pronounced him a likely candidate to one day lead the National Antarctic Expedition he was already planning.

Now, in the spring of 1899, the two met accidentally in London while walking near Buckingham Palace, and Markham, informing Scott that the expedition was at long last about to become a reality, urged him to apply for its command. Scott was at first hesitant. He did not care for ice and snow, had no yearning to become an explorer, and seriously doubted his ability to lead such a serious undertaking. But he felt a need to prove himself, his family situation was still desperate, and after several days of agonizing he filed his application. One year later, over the strenuous objections of several of Markham's associates who felt that a renowned scientist and not an unseasoned young officer should lead Great Britain's first full-scale Antarctic expedition, Robert Falcon Scott received the coveted appointment, and with it a promotion to commander.

For the next thirteen months Scott worked nonstop preparing for the awesome undertaking that lay ahead. He took a course in magnetism; he traveled abroad to study the design of a ship that had recently returned from the polar regions; he interviewed and hired the crew that would serve under his command. In addition, he purchased sleds and the dogs to pull them, ordered the vast quantities of food, clothes, and equipment the members of his expedition would require for the year or more they would be away, familiarized himself with the extensive scientific apparatus they would be taking with them, and tirelessly sought out, through books, journals, and personal interviews with explorers who had already been there, all that was then known about "the bottom of the world."

Finally, after a year of exhausting preparation, Scott took command of the *Discovery*—the ship especially built for the expedition—and on December 21, 1901, he and a crew of forty-six men sailed for the Antarctic. Though they were soon navigating their way past enormous icebergs—some more than five miles long— and drifting pack-ice was constantly bumping and grinding against the ship's sides, they made better time than Scott had expected. In two weeks they had crossed the Antarctic Circle, in three days they had sighted land, and after a few days of reconnoitering they set up base camp at McMurdo Sound, an inlet some nine hundred miles north of the South Pole.

Winter in the Antarctic begins in late April and until then Scott busied himself overseeing short practice trips to test camping equipment, to familiarize his men and himself with their sleds and dogs, and, most important, to lay in depots of food and supplies that would be essential to their explorations come spring. The four months of winter, totally devoid of sunlight, were spent trying to keep warm in a climate where temperatures frequently drop below $-50°$ F. and winds of 100 miles per hour are commonplace. During this period, Scott, making his plans, decided that as soon as the weather allowed he and two others would attempt to cross the Great Ice Barrier—a vast plateau of indeterminate width which no one until then had traversed—and proceed as far south as they could. For this journey he chose the boat's assistant surgeon, thirty-year-old Dr. Edward Wilson—a gifted amateur artist and naturalist and, like Scott, an indefatigable worker—and twenty-eight-year old Ernest Shackleton, a Merchant Navy officer with a zest for adventure who from the start had impressed Scott with his initiative, energy, and intelligence.

On September 23, 1902, having written their farewell letters—Wilson to his wife, Shackleton to his fiancee, Scott to his mother—the three of them set off. Officially their objective was to find what lay beyond the Great Barrier and return to camp by the end of January. But their unstated goal—one that Scott fervently hoped to realize—was to plant their country's flag at the South Pole itself.

From the start, however, virtually everything went

wrong. The snow proved too soft for rapid travel, ice clogged the runners of their sleds, and their dogs, so promising upon leaving camp, almost immediately began to tire and weaken. Scott tried "relaying"—each sled taking half its normal load, and then returning for its other half—and when this proved insufficient he, Wilson, and Shackleton pulled along with the dogs. But even so the dogs' condition continued to deteriorate. By the time the source of the problem was finally discovered—the dried fish they were using as dog food had gone bad—there was nothing they could do but drive the stricken animals as long as they held up and then take over the full hauling themselves.

The terrible suffering of the poisoned dogs, having to watch them struggle on in their agonized state, had a profound effect on Scott and years later was to lead to a decision that would calamitously affect his final expedition. Now, instead of destroying the sick animals, he tried desperately to save them and in doing so fell hopelessly behind schedule. By Christmas Day most of the dogs had been lost, Shackleton was showing the first signs of scurvy, while Wilson, who had removed his goggles to make sketches, was suffering from snow-blindness so acute that even cocaine could not alleviate the pain (his eyeballs, he reported later, had felt as though they were being pierced by red-hot needles). On December 31, a weary, disappointed Scott was forced to order a halt to their march. In ninety days his party had advanced three hundred miles farther south than any man had gone before, but they were still nearly five hundred miles from the Pole, and there was not even a remote chance now of reaching their hoped-for objective.

They headed back none too soon. On their return journey Shackleton's scurvy had grown so pronounced that he began to spit blood, while Wilson was once more

suffering from snow-blindness and was forced to proceed blindfolded. He and Scott were now each hauling
loads that weighed nearly three hundred pounds. "It is
difficult to describe the trying nature of this work,"
Scott noted with characteristic understatement. "We are
as spent as three persons can be."

By January 18, Shackleton was so weak that he had to
be carried by sled. Bad weather further slowed their
progress across the vast, unmarked Barrier and a
number of times they lost their way. Finally, ten days
later, they reached their main depot, and on February 3
they saw specks in the distance that turned out to be a
search party come to meet them. Several hours later
they were back on the *Discovery* where a celebration was
held in their honor. Scott's relief at having managed to
lead his companions back to safety was immense. His
failure to reach the Pole was masked by a stoicism so
deeply rooted that for a time he succeeded in hiding his
disappointment even from himself.

Returning to England, he found the reaction to the
expedition mixed. Markham was ecstatic over "so great
a harvest of scientific results," and an exhibition of
photographs and some of the sledding equipment that
had been used drew ten thousand eager viewers on its
first day. But although as a result of Scott's efforts a
new land had been discovered, the Barrier surveyed,
invaluable scientific data gathered, and a superb collection of fossils, rocks, and animals brought back, Scott
received only scant official commendation. Partly this
was the result of jealousy and intrigue within the
scientific community. But there was another reason:
whatever Scott's achievements—and few denied they
were impressive—he had returned from the Antarctic
minus the single prize the majority of his countrymen
thought worth grasping.

While in his interviews and lectures Scott questioned

the importance of planting the British flag on a barren spot undifferentiated from any other save for its coordinates on a map, while he insisted that his sole wish now was to resume his naval career, public sentiment soon began to mount to return him to the Antarctic and provide him with another opportunity to "get" the Pole.

Over the next few years, Scott himself gradually came to share this objective. Although he had now been advanced to the rank of flag captain and a book he wrote about the expedition—*The Voyage of the Discovery* —was a critical success, his finances remained precarious, he still yearned to "make a mark," and as the hardships of the first expedition faded into the past, the Antarctic with its icy grandeur and the challenge it still offered began to exert an ever-increasing pull on him.

He had begun to sound out members of the *Discovery* crew and was already exploring ways to raise funds when, in February 1907, Shackleton unexpectedly announced plans of his own: he, too, was preparing to try for the Pole, but, unlike Scott, had already secured the necessary financing. Scott, though he attempted to hide his feelings, was deeply wounded. A subordinate he had lifted from obscurity by selecting him for his march on the Pole was about to repay him by making the attempt himself. It was "not playing the game," Scott pointed out with characteristic restraint in a letter he wrote to a friend, for Shackleton to propose an expedition "until he had ascertained that I had given up the idea of going again." Wilson—who concurred with this judgment and turned down Shackleton's repeated invitations to accompany him—helped work out an agreement by which Shackleton promised not to use McMurdo Sound as his base. That was as much of a concession as Shackleton was willing to make. For Scott there was nothing to do now but wait and see how his former lieutenant fared.

The news of Shackleton's expedition that finally reached London in March 1909 was—from Scott's point of view—discouraging but not disastrous. Scott was distressed to learn that Shackleton had broken his word—blaming impassable ice, he had set up base camp at McMurdo Sound after all. Even more unsettling were the results of Shackleton's march: by dint of superhuman effort, he had succeeded in planting his flag within a hundred and eighty miles of the Pole—three hundred miles closer than Scott—and when he returned home it was to a hero's welcome and a knighthood. But like Scott before him, Shackleton had fallen short of his ultimate goal—the South Pole remained unconquered—and now it was Scott's turn to try again.

Scott, while excited by the prospect, was secretly apprehensive about his ability to rise to the challenge. He was now forty-two years old, more self-questioning than ever, and in addition to his mother and three sisters he now had a wife and child to support. In the fall of 1907—about the time that Shackleton had been preparing to sail for the Antarctic—Scott, a confirmed bachelor, had met a twenty-eight-year-old sculptress named Kathleen Bruce and fallen passionately in love. Within days of their meeting he was bombarding her with notes that rhapsodized about her "dear blue eyes" and "sweet tangled head." Within a month he had proposed marriage and, to his delight, been accepted.

Bursting with energy and initiative—traits that Scott greatly admired and was convinced he lacked—Kathleen seemed the perfect foil for his own brooding nature. Sunnily extroverted, she had, while still in her teens, hiked barefoot through the mountains of Italy and Greece, had studied sculpture in Paris, and numbered among her many friends such colorfully controversial figures as Isadora Duncan and Auguste Rodin. Though she affected the dress and manner of a bohemian, steel-willed Kathleen had insisted on remaining chaste until she found a mate "worthy to be the father of my son." It took her only a few days after meeting Scott to decide that in this "decent, honest, rock-like naval officer" she had at long last found a worthy candidate.

Scott, for his part, was charmed and inspired by Kathleen's unblinkingly positive view of life. "Tell me that you *shall* go to the Pole!" she insisted with perfect seriousness. "What's the use of having energy and enterprise, if a little thing like that can't be done." But even Kathleen could not keep Scott's demons at bay for long. Gradually the frequent letters he sent her from the battleship on which he was stationed began to reveal the "dark," despairing side of his nature. "I don't think I'll ever be good enough," he confessed in a typical correspondence. "I'm obstinate, despondent, pigheaded, dejected." While in another, the commander who had won and kept the respect of his crew through two arduous Antarctic years described his personality as "a mean, poor thing . . . something that can neither inspire you nor content others . . . that has a tendency to dominate by sheer persistency." With increasing frequency his letters spoke of a mechanical existence . . . failure . . . cowardice . . . unrest . . . poverty always, until even the seemingly imperturbable Kathleen began to reflect his disquietude. "Con dear," she inquired uneasily in response to one of his self-deprecating tirades, "are you still and always an unhappy man? Oh what's the matter, Con? What *is* the matter?"

Nevertheless in September 1908 they were married,

and when a few months later Scott learned the results of Shackleton's expedition, in spite of his anxious self-doubts he was propelled into action. He abhorred having to solicit money, and it took him a year of incessant lecturing and touring to raise the funds necessary to finance the expedition (with Markham no longer its president, the Royal Geographical Society this time contributed a mere five hundred pounds). By July 1, 1910, all was ready. A converted whaling ship, the *Terra Nova,* had been bought and refitted, the necessary supplies and equipment purchased (this time, in place of sled dogs Scott had decided to rely primarily on ponies), and, most important, a first-rate crew had been assembled, among them a number of men who had sailed with Scott aboard the *Discovery* nine years earlier.

The expedition began in high spirits. "My companions are delightful," Scott wrote enthusiastically to his mother, and before long all aboard the *Terra Nova* were referring to him affectionately as "The Owner." The itinerary called for brief stops at South Africa, Australia, and New Zealand, and at each port of call Scott continued his fund raising, gave lectures and interviews, and attended an endless round of social functions with Kathleen (they were now the parents of a nine-month-old son, Peter, whom Kathleen had left behind so that she could accompany her husband as far south as possible). With reporters Scott was characteristically modest. He was hopeful that the expedition would succeed. He would do everything in his power to see that it did so. He could not, however, entirely rule out the possibility of failure or, for that matter, loss of life. Much, he stressed, would depend on "providence and luck." The newsmen, impressed by Scott's quiet determination and the fervent enthusiasm of his crew, sent back glowing stories explaining that it was now only a matter of time before Commander Scott, and through him England, would lay claim to the South Pole.

It was in this spirit of optimism that the *Terra Nova* reached Australia. There, among the mail waiting for Scott, was a seven-word telegram as unexpected as it was brief. It read: "Beg leave inform you proceeding Antarctic." It was signed "Amundsen."

Scott was familiar with the name and the formidable reputation attached to it. Roald Amundsen was a fearlessly enterprising Norwegian explorer who at the age of twenty-one had abandoned his medical studies to ship out on a voyage to the Arctic, had been the first man to sail through the legendary Northwest Passage, and might have been first at the North Pole had not Robert Peary beaten him to it. With that prize gone, Amundsen had set his sights on the pole that still remained, and two months after the *Terra Nova* sailed from England, Amundsen, in a small borrowed ship, the *Fram,* had left Madeira, Portugal, ostensibly headed back to the Arctic. So cloaked in secrecy had been his preparations that until Scott received his telegram, no one, including the *Fram's* owner— a friend and admirer of Scott's who would never have loaned Amundsen the ship had he known his true intentions—had any inkling of Amundsen's actual destination.

As always, Scott did his best to hide his feelings. In an interview with reporters he made light of Amundsen's telegram, saying he was eager to send one back only he didn't know where to send it. He doubted that the Norwegian would be able to reach the Antarctic in the tiny *Fram.* But whether Amundsen succeeded or failed, he, Scott, would continue to follow the plans he had already prepared, and on November 29, 1910, with Kathleen and the wives of several of the other crew members watching from a tug, the *Terra Nova* left New Zealand and headed for the Antarctic.

Unlike the *Discovery* voyage a decade earlier, this time there were difficulties from the start. Violent storms scattered supplies and washed sleds and ponies overboard. The pumps failed and a flooded engine room had to be bailed out by hand. And no sooner had the skies cleared than they encountered seemingly endless pack ice. It took them twenty days to traverse an ice belt that proved to be four hundred miles wide, and when they finally landed at McMurdo Sound in January 1911 they were nearly a month behind schedule.

On February 2, Scott and a dozen men set out to lay supply depots in preparation for the march toward the Pole. Scott's hope was to plant supplies as far south as the 80° parallel, but blizzards, drifting snow, and a disappointing performance on the part of the ponies slowed their course. On February 17, with the Antarctic winter fast approaching, Scott saw no alternative but to turn back. He ordered the laying of the final and largest store of supplies—a huge cache of food, fuel, and clothing that was dubbed the One Ton Depot—and then the supply-laying party headed back to camp.

Waiting for Scott upon his return was a communication from one of his officers more startling than the telegram that had reached him in Australia. During Scott's absence the *Terra Nova* had made a reconnoitering expedition along the Great Barrier and in an inlet called the Bay of Whales had spotted the *Fram*. Not only had Amundsen effected a successful ocean crossing but he and his men were in excellent health, high spirits, and in possession of the sturdiest, best-trained dogs Scott's people had ever seen. More disquieting yet, by setting up camp on the Barrier itself, Amundsen had placed himself sixty miles closer to the Pole than Scott.

"There is no doubt," Scott noted in a journal that was intended for no eyes but his own, "that Amundsen's plan is a very serious menace to our's." Now, much as he dreaded the thought, there would be a race, the entire world would be watching, and although to reach the Pole meant that close to a thousand miles of the earth's most inhospitable terrain would have to be traversed under indescribably torturous conditions, all acclaim would go to the man who reached the Pole first. "The future is in the lap of the gods," Scott noted philosophically on the last page of the journal he left at camp. "I can think of nothing left undone to deserve success."

On November 1, he set out for the Pole with nine men, four of whom would accompany him on the final leg of the journey. He had wished to start sooner but the weather had been too cold for the ponies, and now as they headed southward two things were soon painfully evident: they were encountering an unusual amount of snow for this time of year, and the decision to use ponies had been a disastrous mistake.

Although Scott had ostensibly chosen the ponies because of the superior pulling power they had displayed during Shackleton's expedition, the truth was that he had never forgotten the agonizing deaths of his dogs nine years earlier. Like many people who have difficulty acknowledging their own pain, Scott could not bear to witness the suffering of helpless animals, and the food-poisoning episode had been a nightmare for him. Logic told him that there was virtually no chance of the incident's repeating itself. But it was not logic that was at issue here. When the time had come to choose, he had opted for ponies.

Now, as blizzard followed blizzard and the heavier ponies sinking up to their bellies in the fresh snow began to weaken and die, Scott spent sleepless nights brooding over his miscalculation. "A hopeless feeling descends on one," he noted in his diary, "and is hard to fight off."

By December 9 they had had to shoot the last of the ponies, and a few days later when Scott named the first returning party it was with instructions that they bring dog teams to meet him and the men who would be accompanying him to the Pole. "We are struggling on . . . against odds," Scott reported in a brief letter he sent back to his wife. Then, attempting not to sound overly pessimistic, he added, "We ought to get through."

On January 3, 1912, three more members of the party were sent back and now there was just Scott and the four men he had chosen for the final march. These were thirty-nine-year-old Dr. Edward Wilson, Scott's oldest, most trusted associate; twenty-seven-year-old Navy Petty Officer Edgar Evans; Lieutenant Henry Bowers, twenty-six, of the Royal Indian Marine; and at the very last moment, wishing all branches of the service to be represented at the Pole, Scott had added a thirty-two-year-old army captain, L. E. G. Oates. Scott, the oldest of the group, was forty-three. "Our five people are perhaps as happily selected as it is possible to imagine," Scott observed in his journal, and for the moment few would have challenged his opinion. "Taff" Evans was an ox of a man who had never been sick a day in his life. Bowers was a "perfect treasure," a brilliant organizer who saw to every logistical detail of the expedition. If not for Oates's superb handling of the ponies and sleds, they would never have gotten this far. "A last note from a hopeful position," Scott wrote Kathleen in the final letter he would be able to send until he returned to camp. "I think it's going to be all right."

On January 6 they were past the point where Shackleton had been forced to turn back. By January 10 they were less than a hundred miles from the Pole. It was becoming an effort to sustain marches in "the double figures," but if they could do so for a few more days, they were almost certain to get through. Most encouraging was the absence of any signs of Amundsen. "What castles one builds," Scott wrote in his journal, "now hopefully that the Pole is ours."

But they were beginning to tire. Evans had cut his hand while preparing food and at subfreezing temperatures the wound would not heal. With the ponies gone they were hauling the sleds themselves and as their energy decreased they began to feel the effect of the cold. "Oh, for a few fine days," Scott lamented. "It is going to be a close thing."

Nevertheless they pressed on. On January 15 the sun came out, they advanced fourteen miles, and Scott was able to write: "It is wonderful to see that two long marches will land us at the Pole . . . it ought to be a certain thing now." The next morning they made equally good progress and were in a jubilant mood when they paused for lunch. Only a storm could keep them from the Pole the following day. Then, in the second hour of their afternoon march, Bowers's sharp eyes detected what looked like a black speck on the horizon. Soon the others saw it as well. In a region of the world where all is white, it could mean only one thing. When they reached it they found it to be a tattered flag. Nearby were the remains of a camp, the area crisscrossed with sled and ski tracks and the imprints of dogs' paws—many dogs.

"The Norwegians have forestalled us," a grieving Scott wrote that night, "and are the first at the Pole. It is a terrible disappointment, and I am very sorry for my loyal companions . . . all the daydreams must go." And the next night's entry read: "The Pole. Yes, but under very different circumstances than those expected . . . Great God! This is an awful place and terrible enough for us to have labored to it without the reward of priority. Now for the run home and a desperate struggle. I wonder if we can do it."

On the following morning, January 18, two miles from the Pole, they found Amundsen's tent. Inside, on a sheet of paper, were the signatures of Amundsen and four others. The paper was dated December 14, 1911. The Norwegians had beaten them by thirty-three days (by the time Scott found the letter, Amundsen and his men, whisked along on dog-pulled sleds, were halfway back to the *Fram*). "Put up our poor slighted Union Jack and photographed ourselves," Scott reported numbly that evening. "Mighty cold work, all of it." In the photograph, for which they posed alongside the Norwegian flag (Bowers setting off the camera shutter with a string), Scott was no longer able to disguise his emotions; his exhausted, weather-blackened face was contorted with grief.

The next morning they began their return journey. Now, with their morale shattered, each day's march seemed an endless agony. The nails were beginning to come off Evans's festering hand and he was having difficulty keeping up with the others. The cold weather was beginning to turn colder still, and tired and short on rations, they chilled easily and had to make camp early. "Is the weather breaking up?" Scott wondered. "If so, God help us." And three days later: "We are slowly getting more hungry . . . a long way to go, and, by Jove, this is tremendous labor."

On February 7, about to descend from the summit, they collected thirty-five pounds of fossil-embedded rocks from the head of Beardmore Glacier. Wilson thought them a remarkable find—important enough to warrant hauling back to camp for examination by the expedition's geologist—and though it meant extra work for men already strained beyond endurance, Scott and the others concurred.

On the way down the glacier they had the worst experience of the trip so far—they lost their way and for two days circled aimlessly among the fog-enshrouded ice. Worse yet, Evans had fallen during the descent, injuring his head, and by the time they reached bottom he had difficulty staying on his skis. For the next few days he struggled to keep up; then, on February 17, the others found him kneeling in the snow, muttering to himself, a wild look in his eyes. By the time they got him into camp Evans was in a coma. When he died later that night, they were still 430 miles from the *Terra Nova*.

Detained by Evans, they had fallen seriously behind schedule and were now forced to travel on severely restricted rations. "Things look very black indeed," was Scott's entry for March 4. "We cannot afford to save food and pull as we are pulling . . . shall we get there?" As fatigue continued to slow their progress, he made the following calculation: "Know that 6 miles is about the limit of our endurance now. We have 7 days food and should be about 55 miles from One Ton Camp . . . $6 \times 7 = 42$. . . ." At their present rate, he calculated, they would run out of food and fuel thirteen miles short of their objective.

Meanwhile, the weather was deteriorating with every passing day. Temperatures of $-40°$ and below were now a daily occurrence. "No idea there could be temperatures like this at this time of year," wrote Scott. "My companions are unendingly cheerful, but we are all on the verge of serious frostbites, and though we constantly talk of fetching through I don't think any of us believes it in his heart."

Oates was the next to weaken. For days, without a word of complaint, he had been trudging along on frozen feet. Now, his toes black with gangrene, the "Soldier" could march no longer. Aware that he was holding up the others, he asked to be left behind. Scott refused. Oates pleaded. Scott was adamant. On the morning of March 17, while a blizzard raged outside their tent, Oates performed an act of gallantry that would soon grace the pages of English history books: announcing offhandedly that he was stepping outside, he stumbled out into the storm and never returned. The next day Scott's own right foot went—nearly all the toes. "These are the steps of my downfall," Scott ruefully noted. Two days earlier he had possessed the best feet of the group. Now amputation of at least one of them was the best he could hope for.

By the evening of March 19, he, Wilson, and Bowers had struggled their way to within eleven miles of One Ton Depot. More than a thousand pounds of food, fuel, and clothing lay tantalizingly near; on their outward journey the distance would have represented no more than a half day's march. But they were barely crawling now and the next morning, March 20, they awoke to a raging snowstorm that kept them pinned inside their tent. Their only hope now was for Wilson and Bowers to try to reach the depot as soon as the storm eased. If they succeeded, they would bring back food and warm clothing for Scott. But the storm raged on. "Blizzard as bad as ever," Scott wrote the following day. "Tomorrow last chance."

For eight more days the gale-force blizzard continued to buffet the tent and between March 23 and 29 Scott made no further entries in his journal. Instead, conserving what little energy he had left, he wrote letters of farewell. Ten years earlier, during the *Discovery* expedition, he had described the difficulty of writing in the cold, "especially when the light was uncertain and the tent was being shaken by the wind . . . some time the breath would form a film of ice over the paper causing the pencil to skid. . . ." Now, bundled up in his sleeping bag alongside the dying Wilson and Bowers, the man who had always disparaged his own stamina and determination wrote to the mothers and wives of his four companions, to his own wife and mother, to friends and associates, and even to the public at large.

When one reads the dozen letters he composed it is difficult to believe the circumstances under which they were written, and harder still to realize they are the work of a dying man. His much admired Message to the Public speaks in eloquent, almost poetic prose of the fortitude of his brave little group:

> We took risks, we knew we took them . . . and therefore we have no cause for complaint, but bow to the will of providence. . . . Had we lived, I should have had a tale to tell of the hardihood, endurance, and courage of my companions which would have stirred the heart of every Englishman. . . .

Wilson's wife he reassured with the observation that even at the end her husband's eyes had a "comfortable blue look of hope." To his friend the playwright J. M. Barrie, he offered a comforting post mortem: "I may not have proved a great explorer, but we have done the greatest march ever made and come very near to great success."

But it is only in his letter to Kathleen (he began it "To

my wife," then substituted the word *widow)* that his doubting, anguished self shows through. Urging her to bring up their son to be a more "strenuous man" than himself ("I had to force myself into being strenuous, you know—had always an inclination to be idle"), he asks her "to take the whole thing very sensibly, as I am sure you will," tries to minimize his own terrible suffering ("I leave the world fresh from harness and full of good health and vigour"), and then can contain his pain no longer. "I have taken my place throughout, haven't I?" he poignantly entreats her, even now, in death, unsure of his achievement. "What lots and lots I could tell you of this journey . . . what tales you would have had for the boy, but oh, what a price to pay."

On March 29, in a faltering hand, Scott made the final entry in his journal. "Outside our door it remains a scene of whirling drift," he wrote. "I do not think we can hope for any better things now. We shall stick it out to the end, but we are getting weak, of course, and the end cannot be far. It seems a pity but I do not think I can write more." Then, having signed his name, he added in a barely legible scrawl: "For God's sake, look after our people."

When a search party from the *Terra Nova* found the tent eight months later, Wilson and Bowers were bundled up in their sleeping bags looking as though they were asleep. Scott had not died so easily. Almost as if begging death to take him, he had thrown back the flaps of his sleeping bag and torn open his coat. His face was pinched and yellow. He was terribly frostbitten, especially his hands, from which he had removed his gloves.

After a brief burial service during which Scott's favorite hymn, "Onward Christian Soldiers," was sung, the tent was collapsed over the bodies, a snow cairn erected above the tent, and a cross made of skis planted on top. An improvised In Memoriam plaque was affixed at the foot of the cross. Naming Scott, Wilson, and Bowers, "who died on the return from the Pole, March 1912," it ended with the following inscription:

> To strive, to seek, to find,
> and not to yield.

Inside this snowy tomb atop the Great Ice Barrier, Scott and his two comrades lie to this very day.

ISADORA DUNCAN

In the winter of 1913, while on a dance tour of Russia, Isadora Duncan, who believed in premonitions, had a bizarre vision. As she was traveling by sled early one morning, she was startled to see rows of children's coffins flanking the road. On closer examination, the coffins turned out to be mounds of snow, but Isadora was so affected by this hallucination that at the end of her recital that evening, she asked her pianist to play a composition she had never previously performed to— Chopin's Funeral March—and on the spot improvised a dance to match its grieving mood. "I danced a creature who carries in her arms her dead," she wrote years later, describing the experience, "with slow, hesitating steps towards the last resting place. I danced the descent into the grave and finally the spirit escaping from the imprisoning flesh and rising, rising towards the Light—the Resurrection."

Until the time of this unsettling incident, Isadora Duncan had scarcely given death any thought. As renowned for her unconventional persona as for her revolutionary approach to dance, blessed with boundless beauty, energy, and genius, she seemed to all who knew her the very embodiment of life. Perhaps that was why the dance of death she improvised in response to her awful vision ended on a note of rebirth. Whatever the reason, both themes were to prove uncannily prophetic. For Isadora was shortly to be visited by a personal tragedy so shattering that for a time her own survival seemed in doubt. Yet in the face of it—and throughout the succession of calamitous events that were to follow—so indomitable was her spirit, so tenacious her commitment to her art, that in the end, even the senseless accident that would kill her would become transformed into a legendary symbol of her aliveness.

The woman whose exuberance even death could not still had been born in San Francisco on May 27, 1878, the youngest of four children, to Irish-American parents with bohemian inclinations—a footloose journalist father who dabbled in poetry, a mother who played the piano—and from her earliest years, Isadora had worshiped at the shrines of Art and Beauty. At the age of six she was teaching neighborhood children to wave their arms about in what she proudly dubbed "my first school of dance." At ten she was helping to support her family—the father had abandoned them years earlier—by instructing adults in the latest ballroom steps. While by her late teens, experimenting with the responses of her own body to emotional and sensory stimuli, a self-taught Isadora had begun to evolve a spontaneous approach to movement that in time would become one of the key foundations of modern dance. "I have discovered the dance," she informed a startled theatrical producer she had come to audition for. "I have discovered the art which has been lost for two thousand years. I bring you the idea that is going to revolutionize our entire epoch."

When Isadora was nineteen, she shocked her first audience by performing a dance she designed to illustrate the verses of Omar Khayyam, costumed in a gauze tunic that bared her beautiful arms to the shoulders and her shapely legs to the knees. When she was twenty, she persuaded her family that fame and fortune awaited them abroad and dragged the penniless Duncan brood off, first to London and then to Paris.

Neither city seemed to know quite what to make of Isadora's "barefoot act" and at first the family was forced to sleep on park benches and warm themselves at local museums. In an effort to earn money, Isadora—who from the start regarded herself not as a dancer but as a sacred vessel for the muses of song and poetry—accepted a job touring with an all-female dance troupe, and while performing in Vienna, caught the eye of a Hungarian impresario who, captivated by her beauty and her remarkable spontaneity of movement, offered her a series of solo concerts in a Budapest theater. It was here that Isadora experienced her first triumph—dancing with fiery abandon to the music of Liszt and Strauss, she played to sold-out houses for thirty successive nights—and launched a career that over the next two decades was to establish her as one of the most celebrated performing artists of her time.

It was also in Budapest that Isadora had her first love affair. From childhood on she had had a passionate weakness for handsome men. At eleven she had fallen madly in love with an "amazingly beautiful" chemist; at eighteen the object of her feverish affections had been a forty-five-year-old Polish poet. But neither these nor her numerous other infatuations had been physically consummated. Now, aglow with success, and feeling the first awareness of her body as "something other than an instrument to express the sacred harmony of music," the twenty-four-year-old Isadora gave herself to a celebrated Hungarian actor as confidently virile as he was attractive ("He assured me I would finally know what heaven was on earth"), and began a series of tempestuous love affairs that were to subject her to notoriety and scandal for the remainder of her life.

But although Isadora was to remain to the end irresistibly attracted to beautiful men, when forced to choose between Love and Art, she invariably chose the latter. Sobered by her mother's disappointing marriage, finding that those men who proposed to her invariably insisted that she give up her dancing, she had vowed early on that she would never wed, even if made pregnant by a lover. So firmly did Isadora adhere to this decision that within a few years of her Budapest debut she found herself the mother of two children, both not only born out of wedlock but fathered by different men.

The father of the first was Gordon Craig, son of British actress Ellen Terry, who at the time of their meeting—he had come to see whether the furor over Isadora's "new" form of dance was justified—was already famed for his own revolutionary innovations as a stage designer and director ("You are marvelous! You are wonderful!" he informed Isadora after her performance. "But why have you stolen my ideas?"). That same night Craig took her to his unfurnished studio, whose black-waxed floor was covered with artificial rose petals, and there they made love. "Here stood before me brilliant youth, beauty, genius," Isadora recalled years later. "Here I found an answering temperament worthy of my metal. In him I had met the flesh of my flesh, the blood of my blood."

But although Craig proved a passionate lover and brilliant companion (to her dying day Isadora insisted that of all the men in her life she had loved him best), she soon discovered to her great disappointment that Craig believed there was room only for one active genius in their relationship. Accordingly, when in the winter of 1906 Isadora learned she was pregnant, she began to set aside as much of her earnings as she could, forced herself to give recitals until her fifth month, and then retired to a little cabin on the North Sea where, alternately elated and depressed by the prospect of impending motherhood ("this fearful monstrous task which had fallen to me; this maddening, joy-giving, pain-giving mystery"), she awaited the arrival of her child.

Finally, in late September, after two days and nights of agonizing labor, a twenty-eight-year-old Isadora gave birth to a blue-eyed, golden-haired girl "formed like a Cupid." For all the anxiety of the past months, Isadora was ecstatic about "this soul . . . which answered my gaze with such apparently old eyes—the eyes of Eternity—gazing into mine with love." Craig, who had always been enamored of the Celtic strain in Isadora, suggested they name the baby Deirdre—beloved of Ireland—and shortly thereafter left Isadora for another woman.

Isadora's second child, born four years later, was the product of a relationship that was to prove equally intense and short-lived. But unlike the gifted but penniless Craig, her partner in this union was a millionaire many times over. His name was Paris Eugene Singer, he was an heir to the Singer sewing machine fortune, and when a debt-ridden Isadora met him in the summer of 1909 (although now in considerable demand as a performer and commanding sizeable fees, she was being bankrupted by one of the many dance schools she struggled to found throughout her life), the handsome, bearded, forty-two-year-old Singer must have seemed a storybook prince come to save her. "I admire your art and your courage," he announced on being admitted to her dressing room. "You have done a great work. You must be tired. Now let it rest on my shoulders." He transported Isadora and her small army of pupils to his villa on the Riviera where the children, attired in light-blue tunics, danced under orange trees, their hands filled with blossoms and fruit.

At first Isadora was content to worship her Croesus-like benefactor at a distance, "in an almost spiritual fashion." But by the fall of 1909 Isadora once again found herself with child, and the following May, in Singer's opulent Riviera retreat, just weeks short of her

thirty-second birthday, Isadora gave birth to a beautiful, blond, blue-eyed boy she named Patrick.

Although Singer saw to it that the baby received the
finest possible care and provided Isadora with her own
suite of rooms at a fashionable hotel and her own
chauffeured limousine, when shortly after Patrick's
birth he proposed marriage, Isadora turned him down.
She was extremely fond of Singer, even loved him after
a fashion, but his great wealth and the aggressive way
he used it to gain his objectives made her fearful of
losing her independence.

But if Isadora's temperament made her unsuited for
the role of wife, her affection for her children was
unbounded. She now saw to it that her tours were kept
as short as possible, and when she was not touring, she,
Deirdre, and Patrick were inseparable. In the garden
behind her Paris studio she built the children their own
little house, and there the three of them would play for
hours on end. Frequently she would invite them into
her studio to watch her rehearse and then would sit
enraptured while they performed for her. Deirdre was
soon her best pupil—Isadora was convinced she would
someday carry on her school—while Patrick was even
more of a wonder: refusing to allow Isadora to teach
him how to dance, he had, almost as soon as he could
walk, begun creating dances to melodies of his own.
Patrick, Isadora prophesied, would grow up to be a
great artist who would one day create a new form of
dance and the new music to accompany it.

And then, while traveling through Russia—on one of
her brief concert tours that occasionally took her away
from her children—Isadora had had the vision of the
coffins.

Upon returning to Paris she had continued to perform her unsettling dance of a mother burying her

dead, and although her everyday life was richer and more fulfilling now than ever before, she was unable to shake off an oppressive sense of foreboding. When at last she consulted a doctor, he told her she was suffering from strained nerves and prescribed a rest in the country. Isadora, who at the time had recital commitments in Paris, compromised by moving herself and the children to Versailles, which was quiet and charming and only a few hours from Paris by car.

On their second morning in Versailles, she, Deirdre, and Patrick were breakfasting in bed when the telephone rang. It was Singer, who had just returned from a long vacation and was eager to see the children. He suggested they all lunch together in the city, and Isadora readily agreed. She and the children, accompanied by their nurse, motored into Paris in her rented limousine and met Singer at an Italian restaurant. Singer was so delighted with their company that before the meal was over he had promised Isadora to build her a theater of her own at the very center of Paris.

After this happy reunion, they all went their separate ways—Singer to a play, the children and their nurse back to Versailles, Isadora to her studio where she had a rehearsal scheduled for later that afternoon. "I thought to rest a while," she recounted years later in her memoirs, describing what happened next, "and mounted to my apartment where I threw myself down on the couch. There were flowers and a box of bonbons that some one had sent me. I took one in my hand and ate it lazily, thinking—'Surely, after all, I am very happy—perhaps the happiest woman in the world. My Art, success, fortune, love, but above all, my beautiful children.' I was thus lazily eating sweets and smiling to myself . . . when there came to my ears a strange, unearthly cry. I turned my head. . . . [Singer] was there, staggering like a drunken man. His knees gave way—he fell before me—and from his lips came these words: 'The children—the children—are dead!'"

A terrible freak accident had occurred. The hired limousine driving the children and their nurse back to Versailles had stalled on an embankment overlooking the Seine. The chauffeur had gotten out to crank the motor and had discovered to his horror as it started that he had accidentally left the gear in reverse. Before he could stop the car, it had backed off the embankment and plummeted into the river at a spot where the water was exceptionally deep. By the time the police were able to locate the car and raise it, Deirdre and the nurse were dead. Patrick, who was still breathing faintly, was rushed to a nearby hospital. But before efforts could be made to resuscitate him, he too was dead.

Isadora did not cry until she was taken to see Deirdre's and Patrick's bodies and pressed their waxlike hands in her own. The thought of her beautiful children being devoured by worms horrified her and she requested that they be cremated and their ashes placed in a vault in an ancient Paris cemetery. On the day of the funeral, students, friends, and neighbors decorated the trees outside Isadora's house with flowers and branches of lilac. Isadora, who was opposed to all religious ritual and had refused to have her children baptized, now refused to wear black. In a simple, light-colored dress and sandals she walked alone at the head of the funeral procession, while thousands of Parisians watched and wept.

The death of Isadora's children stirred the hearts of parents throughout the world and she was deluged with letters and telegrams of condolence, but Isadora was inconsolable. "If this sorrow had come to me much earlier in life," she wrote, "I might have overcome it; if much later it would not have been so terrible, but at that moment, in the full power and energy of life, it completely shattered my force and power."

Along with a letter expressing his grief, Gordon Craig had sent Isadora a small envelope containing dried flowers and a brief note urging her to seek salvation through work ("Isadora," it read. "There is much to do"). But although Isadora tried to resume her dancing and teaching, she found she could not and began instead a restless, aimless year of travel. She sailed to the Greek island of Corfu and attempted to resume her life with Singer, who, finding her sorrow more than he could bear, soon left. With one of her brothers she journeyed to Albania to aid refugees driven there by the Balkan war. Next she crisscrossed Italy by car, haunted by recurrent visions in which her children appeared to her so vividly that on one occasion she pursued their running, laughing forms across the length of a deserted beach.

During her wanderings she allowed herself to be made pregnant by a young Italian sculptor whose name she did not know, and the following fall, back in France, she gave birth to a boy. Since the death of her children she had yearned for a baby, hoping that another child might ease her unendurable sense of loss. But by its first evening the infant was gasping for air— long, whistling sighs escaping from its icy lips—and in spite of frantic efforts to save it, it did not survive the night. "In the next room," Isadora wrote, "I heard hammer taps closing the little box which was my poor baby's only cradle. . . . I believe that in that moment I reached the height of any suffering that can come to me on earth, for in that death it was as if the others died again—it was like a repetition of the first agony—with something added."

In an effort to retain her sanity, Isadora forced

herself to resume performing. She accepted an offer to travel to the United States for a series of recitals, undertook a concert tour of South America, and when, in the spring of 1921, Russia's recently installed Soviet government offered to build her a permanent school if she would agree to teach their children, she gratefully accepted.

Isadora's lifelong dream had been to preside over a school where legions of children could absorb her theories and techniques of dance amidst a setting of tranquility and beauty. Shortly after the death of Deirdre and Patrick, Singer had presented her with a chateau ideally suited to house such a school, but unable to remain in a country where she had suffered so much sorrow, Isadora had turned the chateau over to the French government for use as a military hospital. Now, arriving in Moscow, in place of the school the Soviet authorities had promised her, Isadora found herself confronted by a bureaucratic nightmare of delays and evasions (when six months after her arrival a building was finally allocated for her school, it was without the necessary funds to run it), and in a land to which she had come hoping to dedicate herself to a life of unremitting work and service, a frustrated and restless Isadora instead soon found herself embroiled in what was to prove the most tempestuous and destructive of all her many love affairs.

Isadora was forty-three years old when, in December 1921, she was introduced to one of Russia's most gifted poets, twenty-six-year-old Sergei Essenin. Angelically blue-eyed, his head a mass of golden curls, the delicately built Essenin looked even more youthful and innocent than his years. He had, however, already been married twice, was renowned for his heavy drinking and his violent temper, and was reputed to be both a liar and a thief. In spite of these unsavory credentials and the fact that he spoke no language but Russian, Isadora was drawn to him on sight. Essenin recited his poems for her and called her his "'Sidora." Isadora played with his curls and discovered that he reminded her of Patrick. But although in the weeks that followed Isadora grew increasingly fond of Essenin, she had no idea that their relationship would soon draw her into the one commitment she had resisted all her life— marriage.

Yet marry Essenin she did the following spring for reasons that were as much political as romantic. Isadora had decided that the only way to fund her Russian school was for her to earn the money herself by giving concerts abroad. Essenin was eager to accompany her, but the Soviet authorities were unwilling to let their star poet travel to the West—especially to the United States where they had no embassy—unless Isadora offered him the protection of her name. Isadora, fearful that if she left Essenin behind she would lose him to liquor and other women, and convinced that she alone could cure him of his profligate ways, complied, and in doing so destroyed any prospects for the success of her tour.

From the start, a homesick Essenin engaged in monumental drinking bouts, provoked brawls wherever they traveled, and soon acquired the expensive habit of demolishing their hotel rooms. Isadora had hoped to raise the bulk of the money for her school in the United States, but she had not counted on the anti-Soviet sentiment then sweeping America, and Essenin's provocative presence scarcely helped. During several of her key performances, a drunk Essenin, attired in a Cossack's uniform, marched up and down the aisles, waving a red flag and shouting "Long Live Bolshevism!"

Soon much of the tour had to be canceled—a number of American cities officially banned Isadora's appearance—and although an incensed Isadora publicly sided with Essenin ("This is red!" she yelled at one audience, waving a red scarf above her head. "So am I! It is the color of life and vigor!") and defiantly informed the press that she would rather live in Russia on black bread and vodka than remain in an America cursed with materialism ("You know nothing of Food, or Love, or Art. . . . I shall never see you again!"), she was deeply distressed by the failure of her American visit, and was shattered to find upon returning to Moscow that her husband—who, with her encouragement, had spent a considerable part of her earnings on expensive clothes and presents—had been stealing from her throughout the tour.

When Isadora confronted him with this discovery, an indignant Essenin insisted that he was being unjustly accused, cried, got drunk, threatened to beat her, and a few days later ran off with another woman. At the time Essenin abandoned her, Isadora was in her mid-forties, past her prime as a dancer, and lacking the necessary funds not only for her school but for her personal survival. Weary, destitute, dejected, here, logically, Isadora should have ended her career—perhaps her very life—had she allowed her destiny to be guided by logic.

Instead, after a few weeks' rest, she decided to undertake an extensive tour of the Soviet provinces on behalf of her school. When it ran aground because of bad weather, impassable roads, and a rural populace too poor to buy tickets, she organized another tour—this time of a half dozen European capitals, beginning with Berlin. Again bad luck hounded her. Arriving in Berlin she discovered that the contracts covering her performances in that city had been fraudulently drawn and barely provided for her room and board; while the other countries on her itinerary—in retaliation for what they deemed her pro-Soviet activities—refused to grant her entry visas, thus leaving her not only without funds but stranded. "Better get on a plane and come here and save me," she cabled one of her former pupils. "Otherwise you will soon be sending a wreath for my funeral."

But Isadora was far from ready to expire. While several of her American friends collected enough money to get her to Brussels, a handful of her European admirers persuaded the French government that she was not a dangerous foreign agent, and after considerable delay she was readmitted into France. Although she was now forced to live hand-to-mouth and found herself in ever-increasing debt, so imposing still was her personality, so infectious her fervent commitment to dance, that she persuaded the manager of the most elegant hotel on the Riviera to rent her a room at a nominal "artist's rate," appropriated a small abandoned theater nearby which she transformed into a working studio, and was soon giving recitals there on behalf of her school.

On the last day of 1925, as Isadora was preparing to attend a New Year's party, she received the news that her estranged husband, Sergei Essenin, had committed suicide. His death had been characteristically violent and dramatic (having burned much of his writing, he had cut open his wrist, penned a farewell poem with his own blood, and hanged himself) and caused a shocked Isadora to speak of taking her own life ("I am so unhappy myself," she wrote to a friend, "that I often think of following his example, but in a different way. I would prefer the sea"). But even as Isadora brooded about suicide, she was busily hatching endless projects that might yet finance her school. She wrote tirelessly to prospective benefactors and old friends, sought sponsorship from groups as diverse as the French Communist Party and Mussolini's Fascists, dreamed of renting opera houses for gala fund-raising performances, or sharing her vision of dance with thousands of children, perhaps tens of thousands. And the longer her efforts failed to produce results, the more relentlessly she campaigned. "I still feel we may arise and conquer the earth," she wrote to one of her disciples. "But time is going and I am like a wrecked mariner on a desert island yelling for help!"

Isadora was now nearing her fiftieth year. In public she dressed as theatrically as ever, adorning herself with turbans and trailing shawls, golden sandals and loose, flowing dresses. But since her return from Russia she had put on a noticeable amount of weight, and even short rehearsals left her breathless and exhausted. Before dinner and after it was now not uncommon for her to resort to a cocktail or two as a means of keeping up her morale.

In the spring of 1926, Isadora began to write her memoirs. A few years earlier she had haughtily rejected a lucrative offer from a popular magazine to publish her love letters. Now, in desperate need of money, she accepted a meager advance from an American publisher and began work on her autobiography (it was to be published posthumously as *My Life*). Work progressed slowly for she was affronted by her publisher's insistence that she concentrate on her romantic involvements ("Enough of your hifalutin ideas," read a typical cable from New York. "Send love chapters. Make it spicy"), and, stubbornly resisting these injunctions, she dwelled as long as possible on her early years, her travels, and her Art ("I have written twenty thousand words," she joked defiantly to friends, "and I'm still a virgin").

Meanwhile her financial condition continued to grow increasingly desperate. In Nice her hotel was threatening to evict her, while in her studio the electricity had been turned off. There was no wood for the fireplace, and wherever she went she was pursued by creditors. Harassed beyond even her remarkable endurance, she broke down physically: she began to hemorrhage internally, losing vast quantities of blood. Her doctor, fearing for her life, ordered her to remain in bed indefinitely. Her friends, appalled by her ominously mounting collection of bills, pleaded with her to moderate her life-style. But Isadora, though she tried, could not comply with either set of injunctions for long, and as soon as she was ambulatory, resumed living and working on a scale compatible with her temperament.

In the summer of 1927, she decided to give a recital in Paris. In an effort to keep down expenses, she limited herself to a single rehearsal. But when this prompted rumors that she had done so because she was too old and infirm to dance, Isadora expanded what had been intended as a modest program into an arduously ambitious one and at the age of forty-nine gave a performance that proved to be one of the great artistic triumphs of her career.

Returning to her Riviera studio, she began to plan an even more extensive recital. But she was now more disastrously in debt than ever—her Paris concert, though an artistic success, had, as a result of poor promotion, actually lost her money, and one evening, in an attempt to distract herself from her financial worries, Isadora went for a ride.

The car was an open, red Bugatti, an Italian racing car that had caught Isadora's eye the first time she passed the Nice showroom where it stood on display. Isadora, who had always loved fast driving, would pause to admire the car on her daily walks into town, and one day, acting on the suggestion of a friend, she entered the showroom, claimed she was interested in purchasing the Bugatti, and requested a demonstration ride.

That evening, a handsome young Italian mechanic arrived at Isadora's studio to take her for her test drive. Although it was mid-September the weather was chilly, and friends of Isadora's who were spending the evening with her urged her to wear a cape. Isadora, excited by the prospect of speeding through the night with the young mechanic at her side, chose one of her dramatic shawls instead.

As she climbed into the open Bugatti, her young driver offered her his leather jacket, but she refused. *"Adieu, mes amis,"* she called to her friends. *"Je vais à la gloire!"* She flung her shawl over her shoulder, its heavy fringes catching in the spokes of the rear wheel behind her at the same moment that the mechanic engaged the motor. The shawl, as if yanked by some huge, invisible hand, whipped back, snapping Isadora's neck instantly. By the time Isadora's head hit against the side of the door, the blow smashing in her nose, she was dead.

Three days later, on September 19, 1927, in a drizzling rain, a hearse bearing Isadora's coffin slowly made its way through the side streets of Paris. Her friends had wished for the procession to pass through the Champs Élysées, but the American Legion was marching in Paris that day and a circuitous alternate route had to be taken. In spite of the detours and the rain, thousands of weeping mourners followed behind Isadora's hearse, while thousands more waited at the cemetery where fourteen years earlier Isadora had brought the bodies of her children.

At a closing ceremony following Isadora's cremation, Shubert's "Ave Maria" was sung, a Bach aria was played on the violin, and Isadora's ashes were placed alongside those of Deirdre and Patrick. Today, Isadora Duncan, who during her lifetime was denied the permanent school she struggled so hard to establish, is acknowledged as the creator of a new art form and as the first of the great modern dancers. Because of these remarkable achievements and because her life was a testament to integrity, perseverance, and courage, she has influenced and inspired more dancers than even she could have conceived of in her most extravagant dreams.

BENITO MUSSOLINI

CLAD IN HIS FAMILIAR GRAY-GREEN UNIFORM, A black fez crowning his shaved head, he would strut out onto the palace balcony, step triumphantly up on the ledge, and instantly the cry of "Duce, Duce, Duce!" would rise from the tens of thousands thronged below. "Blackshirts of the revolution," he would intone in his commandingly vibrant voice, "men and women of Italy, hear my words. . . ," and for the duration of his speech, those gathered in the square as well as the millions listening throughout the land felt they were in the presence of history. For the jaw-jutting speaker who for two decades held them spellbound with his heady exhortations was Benito Mussolini, the founder of fascism, the first of this century's totalitarian dictators, the self-anointed ruler of "the new Roman Empire."

At home and abroad his very name stirred violent controversy. Adolf Hitler hailed him as his mentor. Franklin Roosevelt denounced him as an infamous backstabber. Winston Churchill likened him to a jackal, while to a famous American journalist he was "the most formidable combination of turncoat, ruffian and man of genius in modern history." Wooing his countrymen with dreams of glory, in the end a victim of his own grandiose delusions, he ruled Italy for more than twenty years, and when at last its war-ravaged people turned against him, his downfall provoked one of the grimmest acts of retribution witnessed in our time.

The son of an impoverished blacksmith, Mussolini was born July 29, 1883, in Dovia, an obscure hamlet in the northern province of Forli. His mother was a pious Catholic, his father a socialist/atheist who named him after the Mexican revolutionary Benito Juarez—a man

famed, ironically, for the execution of an emperor just
two decades earlier. From the start Mussolini displayed
exceptional intelligence coupled with a turbulently
aggressive nature. So quarrelsome was he as a boy, so
prone to violence, that at the age of nine his parents
were forced to send him to a church-run school noted
for its discipline—an institution from which he was
soon expelled for stabbing a classmate with a penknife.

Masking a gnawing sense of inferiority behind a
strutting arrogance that would soon become his trademark, the young Mussolini was driven by a need to
command attention at all costs. He would lead attacks
on teachers, fire off ultimatums to school authorities,
organize student protests, and bathe in the notoriety
these activities earned him. A voracious reader, his
mind aflame with ideas from whatever book he had
read last, he would rant at the walls of his room for
hours at a time, a slight, pale-faced, fiery-eyed boy
rehearsing speeches "for a day when all Italy will
tremble at my words."

It would take him nearly thirty years to achieve his
dream and the road that would carry him to absolute
power would be as violently erratic as Mussolini himself. Surprisingly, the man who would someday head
the first fascist state began his political career not as an
exponent of the Right, but as a police-harassed Socialist
who admired Lenin, treasured a medallion of Karl
Marx, and was arrested for protesting Italy's imperialis-
tic policies. But he could not play the downtrodden
pacifist for long. On the eve of World War I—by then
the leader of the peace wing of the Socialist Party—he
dramatically reversed himself, urged Italy's entry into
the war on the side of the Allies, and was expelled from
the party as a traitor.

When Italy declared war in 1915, he was among the
first to volunteer, fought with exceptional valor, and in

1917, at the age of thirty-four, had his first serious brush with death when a cannon he was firing exploded, riddling his body with more than forty pieces of shrapnel. In a month he underwent twenty-seven operations, all but two performed without anesthetic, the damage to his left leg so severe that for the rest of his life he would be forced to wear zippered boots to keep the leg from becoming inflamed and suppurating.

In 1919, still recovering from his wounds, he presided over the founding of the Fascist Party in Milan, its members mostly disaffected veterans, its name derived from the *fasces,* the bundle of cord-bound rods coupled with an ax that symbolized the office of consul of ancient Rome. By 1921 his candidates had won thirty-four seats in the national Chamber of Deputies. By the following year his party boasted a million members and Mussolini, proclaiming his Fascists a bastion against anarchy and bolshevism, haughtily issued an ultimatum to the government: either it would step down in his favor peacefully, or he would lead a march on Rome and engage it "in a struggle to the death." When the government countered by declaring martial law, he ordered his Blackshirts to march. Converging on Rome from towns and hamlets throughout Italy, his ragtag army entered the capital to a heroes' welcome, the Cabinet hastily resigned, and on October 28, 1922, King Victor Emmanuel appointed thirty-nine-year-old Benito Mussolini as Italy's sixtieth premier.

So began the reign of this bullying, power-hungry leader whose insatiable need to make his will felt continued to grow as rapidly as his power increased. Having gained undisputed control of his own country—a month after his appointment as premier the Chamber of Deputies granted him dictatorial powers—Mussolini was soon looking beyond Italy's borders for fresh fields to conquer. In 1923, over a minor dispute

with Greece, he sent his navy to bombard the unde-
fended island of Corfu. Next it was Ethiopia which his
armies bloodily overran in open defiance of the League
of Nations. Then Spain, where his infusion of men,
money, and arms was instrumental in helping Franco's
rebel forces win the Civil War. Finally, in the late 1930s,
made overconfident by easy victories, he joined with
Hitler in forming the Rome-Berlin Axis—a partnership
that was soon to be instrumental in plunging the world
into World War II.

When the two men had first met in Rome in 1934, it
had been Hitler who stood in awe of his older, more
celebrated Italian counterpart. But by the time Mussolini repaid the visit three years later, their roles had
become reversed. Germany was now the most powerful
nation in Europe, and Mussolini, who above all worshiped might, was enthralled by the rallies, parades,
and war games the Nazis cannily staged in his honor.
Two months after his state visit he followed Hitler's
lead and withdrew from the League of Nations, then
stood by while Hitler annexed Austria (a country whose
independence he had sworn to defend). Temporarily
sobered by the warnings of his ministers who cautioned
that Italy was economically and militarily ill-prepared to
wage war, Mussolini held back while Germany annexed
Czechoslovakia and invaded Poland, but when in June
1940 the armies of the Third Reich overran France, he
could no longer resist the lure of certain victory, and
two days before the fall of Paris he joined in the attack.

It was a triumph he did not savor for long. Striving to
keep up with Hitler's military successes, Mussolini
ordered the invasion of Greece, a job his generals
botched so badly that the scornful Germans were
forced to complete it for them. Almost from the start
his armies in North Africa were routed by numerically
inferior British forces. By 1942, he had been dragged

into war with both Russia and the United States, Italian cities were being bombed, the Americans had joined the British in Africa, and a dispirited Mussolini made fewer and fewer speeches from his famous balcony.

And then, in the summer of 1943, with his soldiers surrendering in alarmingly growing numbers, with home-front morale rapidly crumbling, came the most stunning blow of all: under the leadership of General Mark Clark, a joint Anglo-American force landed in Sicily, the presence of enemy troops on Italian soil setting in motion a chain of events that before long was to cost Mussolini his life.

Ordered by Hitler, on whom militarily and psychologically he now depended more and more heavily, to abandon southern Italy to the onrushing Allies and concentrate on the defense of the north, Mussolini met resistance from his own Council of Ministers who, convinced that *any* further struggle was useless, demanded his resignation as a prelude to their suing for peace. A stunned Mussolini—for all his bombast, when forcefully confronted, he would quickly become immobilized and lost in depression—took his case to King Victor Emmanuel, a pliable figurehead whose support Mussolini had previously always taken for granted. This time, however, the king proved maddeningly evasive (unbeknown to Mussolini, he had already thrown in his lot with the ministers), and as Mussolini left the royal palace he was informed by officers sent by the council that he was being placed in "protective custody." Over the next few weeks he was shunted from one hiding place to another—lest the Germans find him and restore him to power—the last of the hideaways an abandoned ski lodge high in the Italian Alps.

His jailers found the once awesome Duce eerily transformed. The stocky dictator, renowned for his wrestlerlike physique, appeared stooped and haggard, his dark eyes bulging from a pallid, shrunken face. Until recently so vain that he had forbidden any official mention of his age, Mussolini now showed scarcely any interest in his personal appearance. "When a man and his organism collapse," he noted resignedly in his diary, "the fall is irretrievable." Ironically, in one key respect the dictator's imprisonment proved beneficial: he was afflicted with duodenal ulcers, and in recent months gastric attacks had been causing him almost unendurable pain. Now, shorn of all duties and responsibilities, Mussolini experienced relief from his ulcers for the first time in ages, and passed his days chatting with his jailers, reading books on history and philosophy, and making pensive entries in his journal.

On September 8, 1943, the pro-armistice government formed in the wake of his arrest surrendered to the Allies, the Germans retaliated by seizing Rome, and four days later, on personal orders from Hitler, S.S. paratroopers swooping down in gliders rescued Mussolini from his ski-lodge prison and flew him to Germany for an audience with the Fuehrer.

Judging by the reports of those closest to him, Hitler found the interview most distressing. His once arrogantly confident ally was now a sallow, beaten-looking man who seemed ready to relinquish all for the sake of peace and quiet. "The Fuehrer," his aide Joseph Goebbels observed disdainfully, "expected the first thing the Duce would do would be to wreak full vengeance on his betrayers. He gave no such indication, however, which showed his limitations. He is not a real revolutionary like the Fuehrer or Stalin. . . . I have never seen the Fuehrer so disappointed."

Nevertheless, the Fuehrer had plans for his old comrade. Working from within Germany, Mussolini was to hastily rebuild the Fascist Party, then return to Italy and assume control of his new-formed government. Even as a holding action, the move reeked of cynicism on Hitler's part. There was no longer any popular support for facism in Italy. Aware of this, Hitler now regarded it as occupied territory and Mussolini a puppet who would henceforth rule at his bidding.

For the next eighteen months Mussolini's seat of government was not Rome but a villa five hundred miles safely to its north on scenic Lake Garda. Here, a virtual prisoner of the Germans, Mussolini presided over a paper republic, surrounded by a hastily scraped together cabinet of such party hacks as could still be persuaded to serve. Housed nearby were the youngest two of his five children and Rachelle Mussolini, the stout, matronly woman who had been his devoted wife for the past thirty-five years. Ensconced across the lake in a handsomely appointed villa was a woman even more fiercely dedicated to him—his beautiful young mistress, Claretta Petacci.

They had met twelve years before when Mussolini was nearly fifty and Claretta not yet twenty, he at the zenith of his power, she a dark-haired, blue-eyed, strikingly beautiful girl with a husky voice and a sultry smile that men found irresistible. The daughter of a senior Vatican physician, Claretta Petacci had idolized Mussolini since her childhood, sleeping with his portrait under her pillow, sending him impassioned patriotic poems, going so far as to mail him an invitation to her fourteenth birthday party. From their first chance meeting in 1932—their cars passed one another en route to a seaside resort—Claretta, who by then was engaged to a young air force lieutenant, knew she was in love. And this time, miraculously, the object of her worshiping affection reciprocated by inviting her to visit him at his official headquarters, the resplendent Palazzo Venezia in Rome. It was a strangely formal meeting that took place in the dictator's cathedral-sized office, the two of them standing while he first inquired after the health of her family, then questioned her at length about her tastes and hobbies (piano playing, oil painting, skiing, tennis). It might have been an interview between a kindly school principal and a promising new student. Only as Claretta was about to leave did Mussolini mention that because of her he had not slept for three successive nights.

With this restrained, almost timid avowal of his feelings, their relationship began. Mussolini had a reputation for treating his women ruthlessly, and by the time he met Claretta he had had numerous stormy, often brutal, affairs. In his teens he had exercised his will on prostitutes and working girls and his marriage in no way diminished his craving for these harsh sexual conquests. As he had risen to power he had begun to gravitate toward mistresses who were more worldly and sophisticated, but with them as with his earlier bed partners he continued to display a need to dominate at all cost, not infrequently resorting to physical violence to achieve his aim. Only two women were exempted from his lifelong pattern: his wife, Rachelle—whom he respected but did not love—and Claretta Petacci.

From the start he was uncharacteristically solicitous of her. He waited two years after his first meeting with Claretta (time enough for her to marry and separate from her young lieutenant) before inviting her to become his mistress, and even then he first sought the consent of her parents. He discreetly installed her in her own suite at the Palazzo Venezia, and when he took her traveling, he frequently invited her younger sister to accompany them in an effort to protect her from gossip. When state business forced him to travel without her, his "Dear little one" received frequent, doting love letters from her "Beloved Ben," and the one time

Claretta was seriously ill—as a result of an extrauterine pregnancy she had developed peritonitis—he not only remained at her bedside for days on end, but insisted on attending an operation she was forced to undergo. For her part, while Claretta soon realized she had consigned herself to a furtive, lonely life that was spent mostly waiting for Mussolini's all-too-infrequent visits, while she was bitterly jealous of any woman he came in contact with and was herself often restlessly bored, from the time they became lovers she was unwaveringly faithful to him, her dedication to her beloved Duce actually increasing as his fortunes waned.

Now, in the spring of 1945, she was at Lake Garda, a beautiful woman of thirty, renting a house at her own expense to be near her aging, dispirited lover, the only member of Mussolini's retinue who willingly spurned safety to be at his side at the very moment when his life was in jeopardy. For with Allied advances rapidly gaining momentum, more and more Italians were rising up to attack Mussolini's puppet republic from within. In recent months an alliance of various antifascist groups collectively calling themselves the Resistance had openly joined the battle and already controlled scattered areas of the country. As stories filtered into Lake Garda about the bloody retribution that was being visited on even the most lowly Fascist officials by marauding partisan bands, there could be little doubt about the fate that awaited Mussolini and his entourage should they be similarly apprehended.

Meanwhile, although aware that each day he remained at Lake Garda lessened his possibility of escape, Mussolini was torn by indecision. One moment he seemed amenable to Claretta's plan that the two of them seek refuge in the Austrian Alps, the next he would warn her that any talk of defeat was not only premature but seditious, while a short while later he might be heard telling a subordinate that if the end was indeed imminent, he wished to die a leader, commanding his Blackshirts in a glorious last stand.

Finally, in mid-April he bestirred himself sufficiently to travel to Milan, the birthplace of fascism and now the only major city still in government hands. For a week he held court here, listening to the advice of an endless stream of friends and supporters, still vacillating between the desire to save himself and to die fighting, and when he at last decided on a course of action, his decision reflected his continued ambivalence. Under the auspices of the Bishop of Milan, he agreed to a secret meeting with the leaders of the Resistance to learn their terms of surrender for himself and his government. If these proved unacceptable he would almost certainly follow the plan advocated by his fanatical party secretary, Allesandro Pavolini—a final stand with his Blackshirt legions at Val Tellina, a heavily fortified mountain stronghold some hundred miles north of Milan (although, if for some reason, this plan proved unfeasible as well, Val Tellina conveniently offered excellent escape routes both to Germany and Switzerland).

On April 25, 1945, with the Americans on the outskirts of Milan, Mussolini arrived at the bishop's palace for his meeting with the partisans. If he was unprepared for the severity of their terms—full and unconditional surrender within the hour—he was stunned by what they told him next. Behind his back, the German High Command for Italy had already negotiated its own surrender terms, and had even offered to disarm all Italian military units for their Allied captors. Sputtering that before deciding his own fate he must first "settle accounts" with his German betrayers, Mussolini hurried out of the meeting, promising to return within the allotted hour.

But he did neither. Instead, upon reaching his headquarters, he ordered an immediate withdrawal to Lake Como, thirty miles north of Milan. There he would wait overnight for the ten thousand Blackshirts Pavolini had promised to recruit. Then, at the head of this loyal army, he would proceed to Val Tellina.

It was an odd convoy that set out for Lake Como at the very time the partisans' deadline was expiring. At the head of the column in an open Alfa-Romeo sat a grimly defiant Mussolini in full militia uniform, a briefcase bulging with state papers in his lap. Atop the briefcase was a machine pistol a soldier had thrust into his hands as he was departing—a weapon he had not the vaguest idea how to use. Close behind followed a lorry carrying his German bodyguards (on Hitler's orders, they remained at Mussolini's side twenty-four hours a day—both to protect him and to keep him from escaping). Behind the Germans came the cars of Mussolini's ministers. These in turn were followed by trucks crammed with the ministers' possessions (as well as a fortune in looted government gold). And finally, bringing up the rear of this unusual motorcade, was a car with Spanish diplomatic plates. Inside this last car, draped in a sumptuous fur coat, as carefully coiffed and made up as if on her way to some gala event, rode Claretta Petacci.

By ten o'clock that evening, when the cars and trucks finally reached Lake Como, the battle for control of Milan was already under way. Repeated phone calls were made to the beleaguered city in an attempt to learn the size and whereabouts of the army Pavolini had stayed behind to recruit, but no one in Milan seemed to have any concrete information and an alarming number of the strongpoints called were already in enemy hands. For the next several hours a dispirited Mussolini sorted through the government papers he had brought in his briefcase and listened glumly while his ministers argued among themselves as to what should be done next. Finally, at three o'clock in the morning he wearily announced his decision. They would move on to Menaggio, a lake town twenty miles north of Como and only a dozen miles from the Swiss border, and wait for Pavolini and his troops there.

It was raining when they set out. In the heavy downpour it took them nearly three hours to reach Menaggio. Here, several hours later, Pavolini finally caught up with them. As promised he had rounded up an army of Blackshirts, had brought the hastily assembled troops to Como, and had witnessed their confusion and dismay on learning of Mussolini's departure. For the morale of the soldiers, as well as Mussolini's personal safety, he begged Mussolini to stay put until the troops could catch up with him. After a hurried conference it was agreed that Pavolini would return immediately to Como, fetch his Blackshirt brigades, and rendezvous with Mussolini and his ministers in Menaggio by early afternoon.

In the aftermath of the meeting Mussolini's spirits brightened noticeably and for the first time since the departure from Milan a cautious optimism could be discerned among his followers. But as the appointed time came and went and Pavolini failed to return, the mood inside the abandoned hotel where Mussolini and his ministers were waiting became progressively more anxious. Milan Radio, seized that morning by the Committee of Liberation, was issuing bulletins and news reports that grew more ominous by the minute. After a brief but bloody struggle, Milan had been liberated. Throughout Italy tribunals were being established to deal with war crimes. An official proclamation had been drawn up indicting the leaders of fascism. For those guilty of "betraying the country and leading it to its present catastrophe," it demanded the penalty of death.

By midafternoon, amidst much shouting and confusion, the ministers decided that two of them would attempt to cross into Switzerland. If they succeeded and Pavolini had still not returned, Mussolini and the others would follow. But several hours later news reached the hotel that the two ministers had not only been stopped by Italian border guards but arrested, and once more all hope focused on Pavolini and his Blackshirt army.

It was not until after midnight that a dazed and weary Pavolini finally arrived in an armored car, and it took Mussolini several minutes to grasp the news his distraught party secretary brought him. The majority of the troops Pavolini had left behind in Como that morning had subsequently either scattered or surrendered to partisans. Of those that remained he had been able to persuade only a tiny portion to follow him to Menaggio. When Mussolini, looking out the window, asked where the loyal troops were, a shamefaced Pavolini pointed hesitantly to some soldiers clustered around the armored car in which he had arrived. The dedicated army he had promised Mussolini for a heroic last stand at Val Tellina numbered exactly twelve men.

By dawn, the column of vehicles carrying Mussolini and his entourage was on the move again. Now, as they headed still farther north, they joined up with a large convoy of Luftwaffe trucks whose destination was Austria. The procession made slow but steady progress until it was stopped by a partisan roadblock at a mountain village, the name of which, coincidentally, was Musso. Here, a small group of partisans under the leadership of Count Pier Bellini, a young aristocrat turned Resistance fighter, succeeded in bluffing the war-weary Germans into believing that they were vastly outnumbered. A six-hour parley ensued, with the demoralized Germans at last agreeing to the partisans' conditions: all Luftwaffe vehicles and personnel would be allowed to pass; all Italians attached to the convoy would have to remain behind.

During the interminable negotiations, Mussolini had waited with mounting agitation inside the sweltering armored car at the head of the column. With him was Claretta Petacci. Just a few days earlier she had rejected her parents' pleas that she escape with them to Spain. Instead, in her own car, she had followed Mussolini to Milan and from there had accompanied him on his desperate northward exodus. When the motorcade had been stopped by the partisans, she had hastily joined Mussolini inside the armored car where she now sat alongside him holding his hand, attempting to comfort him by her presence.

When at last the parley at the roadblock ended, Mussolini was approached by his German bodyguards and urged to put on an army coat and helmet that would disguise him as a sergeant in the Luftwaffe. Mussolini asked that similar disguises be provided for Claretta and the half dozen ministers who were with him in the truck. When the Germans said they could help only him, Mussolini refused to comply. If he did such a cowardly thing, he protested, he would bear the shame of it for the rest of his life. Suddenly Claretta began to cry. Sobbing hysterically, she begged Mussolini to save himself. For a long moment, a white-faced Mussolini remained motionless. Then, embarrassedly averting his eyes from Claretta, his ministers, and the Germans, he rose and exited from the car.

Following the instructions of his bodyguards, Mussolini donned the coat and helmet they gave him as well as a pair of sunglasses and climbed aboard one of the Luftwaffe trucks, seating himself as far away from its door as possible. When the truck was stopped and boarded he kept his head down pretending to be in a drunken stupor, but the young partisan conducting the search was a former gunner in the Italian navy who, by chance, had seen Mussolini close-up the previous year. Now, scarcely daring to believe what he saw, he hurried to his commanding officer with the news of his find. Climbing aboard the truck, the officer spoke to the drunk soldier in German. Receiving no reply, he addressed him in Italian as "Your Excellency." Still receiving no answer, he bellowed out Mussolini's name. This time the immobile figure slowly raised its head and nodded. With a sigh, a weary Benito Mussolini took off the helmet, undid the coat (revealing his famed militia uniform underneath), and without a word of protest climbed down from the truck.

He was taken to the local town hall where he was briefly interrogated by Count Bellini and then transferred to a nearby police barracks (the safest place to keep him, Bellini decided, until word came from the National Committee of Liberation in Milan as to what it wished done with its illustrious prisoner). When Bellini visited Mussolini at the barracks several hours later, Mussolini asked him if he would kindly deliver a message to one of the other prisoners—"the woman with the fur coat"—informing her that he was safe. It was as a result of this request that Bellini realized that the strikingly pretty woman being held at the town hall must be Claretta Petacci. Promising to deliver the message, Bellini departed. Visibly relieved now that all further decisions had been taken out of his hands, Mussolini spent the remainder of the evening conversing with his guards, who regarded him with awed respect. Commending them for their courteous treatment, he encouraged them to ask questions, then, making use of his oratorical skills, held them spellbound with stories about some of the great historical events he had participated in. Shortly before midnight he retired to a room that had been set aside for him and went to sleep.

At one o'clock in the morning Mussolini was awakened by Bellini, who informed him that as a precautionary measure—to prevent him from falling into the hands of hostile mobs or of Fascist groups that might try to restore him to power—he was being transferred to yet another hiding place: a villa on the outskirts of Como. To keep his identity secret during the transfer he would have to assume yet another disguise—this time one that would allow him to pass for a wounded partisan. An hour later, his head swathed in bandages, Mussolini was hurried through a heavy downpour to a waiting Fiat. As the car sped off into the stormy night, Bellini informed Mussolini that he was about to be reunited with Claretta Petacci, who, upon receiving his message, had begged to be allowed to join him (Bellini had at first refused to grant her request, but an anguished Claretta had pleaded with such tearful insistence that the young partisan chief had at last relented).

Even as Mussolini learned this unexpected news, the headlights of the car picked out another Fiat waiting alongside a small country bridge. In the downpour, Mussolini and Claretta were allowed to climb out and greet each other briefly. Then the two cars proceeded on to Como. As they neared the town, however, gunfire could be heard and Bellini, learning that American troops were in the vicinity, changed his plans and decided to hide Mussolini in the mountain village of Mezzegra instead. A half hour later they had gone as far as their car could take them and were forced to proceed on foot, a mink-draped, high-heeled Claretta slipping on wet stones, while a weary Mussolini, his bandaged head ghostly against the night rain, did his best to keep her from falling.

When at last they arrived at their destination—a rough-hewn, two-story cottage high in the hills—they were offered cups of ersatz coffee by the peasant family that lived there (from whom their identity was withheld), then shown to a small, unheated room on the upper landing whose furnishings consisted of a single bed, a pair of rickety chairs, a table, and some religious pictures on the walls. It was a far cry from the comfort and splendor of the Palazzo Venezia, and as they entered Mussolini remarked that the room reminded him of the one he had been born in. Still, after the rigors of the past two days, both Claretta and he seemed grateful to have a bed in which to lie, and minutes after their partisan guards withdrew, the light inside the room—a solitary bulb dangling from the ceiling—was extinguished.

Late the following morning the farmer's wife brought them food which they ate off a packing case: porridge for Claretta; bread, cheese, and salami for Mussolini. From the window of their room the majestic peaks of Val Tellina could be seen in the distance and for a while Mussolini attempted to distract Claretta and himself by identifying the various mountains. After a short while, however, he lapsed into silence, while Claretta climbed back into bed in her clothes, wrapping the blankets around her to keep herself warm.

Shortly before four o'clock that afternoon the door of their room was thrown open and a mustached man in a brown raincoat rushed in, machine gun in hand. Informing Mussolini and Claretta that he had come to rescue them, he told them they must leave instantly if they wished to be saved. In fact, their "rescuer" was thirty-six-year-old Colonel Walter Audisio, a battle-hardened partisan who had been sent to Mezzegra by the Committee of National Liberation with orders to find Mussolini and his ministers, execute them, and bring their bodies back to Milan (so determined was the committee that the leaders of fascism be brought to justice by their own countrymen, that to throw the Allies off the scent, it had that morning "regretfully" informed them that Mussolini had already been captured and shot).

Now, as a suspicious Mussolini plied their would-be liberator with questions, Audisio brushed his queries aside, insisting there would be time enough to talk when they reached safety. Wary of Audisio, yet desperately wishing to believe that salvation was at hand, a reluctant Mussolini at last agreed to accompany him. With Claretta leading the way, the three of them hurried along a narrow path to a waiting car. As the car started down the mountainside in the rain, Mussolini asked Audisio if he thought his shaved head might be recognized and give him away. Audisio said he doubted it, then, noting that Mussolini seemed dissatisfied with his answer, he advised him to put on his militia cap and pull it down over his eyes.

A mile down the narrow mountain road, the car came to a sharp halt at the Villa Belmonte, a large house surrounded by a high stone wall. Audisio told Mussolini and Claretta to climb out of the car and pointed them toward the gateway. As they entered the courtyard, Audisio announced that by order of the High Command of the Committee of National Liberation, he had been "charged to render justice to the Italian people." As the partisan chief emotionlessly intoned the formal-sounding death sentence, Mussolini stared at him blankly as if not comprehending what was being said. Claretta, however, began to scream hysterically, protesting that he had no right to murder them in cold blood, without so much as a hearing. Audisio, shouting at her to step aside or he would shoot her first, pointed his machine gun at Mussolini and pressed the trigger only to find that the gun had jammed. Over Claretta's continued shrieking, he yelled to one of his subordinates for another gun and the man ran over with the requested weapon—a long-barreled MAS French machine pistol.

As Audisio took hold of this second gun, Mussolini, as if emerging from a dream, unbuttoned his gray-green militia jacket and pulled it back. "Shoot me in the chest!" he ordered. Now that all hope was gone, he sounded almost as assured as in the days of old. But as Audisio fired, Claretta grabbed for his gun and was the first to fall dead, shot through the heart. Then, at almost point-blank range, Audisio fired a burst of nine shots at Mussolini. The first two cut through the dictator's raised forearm, the others lodged in his thigh, collarbone, neck, and aorta. Unlike Claretta, who had fallen instantly, Mussolini slid slowly to the ground. For a moment his body remained propped against the wall, then gradually it collapsed onto the wet cobblestones. He was still breathing when Audisio fired a single shot directly into his heart.

For the next four hours the bodies of Mussolini and Claretta lay side by side, their blood mingling in the rain. At eight o'clock that evening they were loaded into a yellow moving van alongside sixteen members of Mussolini's entourage whom Audisio had rounded up and executed in the meantime. At three in the morning the van reached its final destination—the Piazzale Loreto—a square in Milan where fifteen civilian hostages had been shot by Fascists the previous fall. One by one the bodies were unloaded and dumped in front of a bombed-out gas station, its exposed girders jutting out starkly against the sky. By chance, Mussolini's body was heaped atop Claretta's, and for the remainder of the night he lay with his head cradled on Claretta's white-bloused bosom.

In the morning, the crowds that gathered to view the bodies were at first merely curious. Someone placed a mock scepter in Mussolini's lifeless hand and newsmen busied themselves taking photographs. By nine o'clock, however, the square had filled to overflowing and the handful of partisans guarding the bodies could no longer control the mob. A man forced his way past them and, with a savage kick of his boot that made a hideously crunching sound, caved in the side of Mussolini's skull. Others followed, kicking and pounding at Mussolini's head and body. A woman produced a gun and fired five shots into the dictator—one for each of the sons she had lost in the war. A man lit a torch and tried to set Mussolini's head on fire. Not to be outdone, several women spread their skirts and urinated on his upturned face.

By now the partisan guards were firing warning shots into the air and a high-pressure hose was turned on the mob, but to no avail. A huge man, his shirt smeared with blood, began to lift the bodies, carcass-fashion, above his head, showing them off to the wildly approving crowd. First, Mussolini, his face a pulp but the eyes still open, his left foot still encased in its zippered boot. Then Claretta, her tailored clothes tattered, her hair blood-matted and disheveled, yet, for all that, her face strangely serene. With the crowd howling for more, a rope was tied to Mussolini's ankles and he was hoisted, legs first, up the gas-station girder. Claretta was strung up alongside him in the same fashion, with ghoulish propriety a woman in the crowd securing her skirt to keep it from revealing her undergarments. Four of the other bodies were hung alongside, and there the six of them dangled upside-down throughout the day, while smiling spectators posed for photographs in front of them like proud fishermen in front of a prize catch.

That evening, by order of the Allied authorities, their bodies were at last cut down and Mussolini's battered remains were given a secret burial in the Mosocco cemetery in Milan. A dozen years later his casket was released to Rachelle and her children and, in accordance with Mussolini's wishes, he was buried alongside his son Bruno—a great favorite of his—who had been killed in the war Mussolini had helped precipitate.

Claretta, too, ultimately received her own modest monument. At the gate of the Villa Belmonte—the very spot where she died with her "beloved Ben"—stands a small marble cross. Its simple inscription reads:

Clara Petacci

April 28, 1945

ZELDA FITZGERALD

I don't want you to see me growing old and ugly.
I know you'll be a beautiful old man—romantic
and dreamy—and I'll probably be most prosaic
and wrinkled. We will just *have* to die when we're
thirty.

—Zelda Sayre, nineteen, to her
fiancé, F. Scott Fitzgerald

I refer to the [Flapper's] right to experiment with
herself as a transient poignant figure who will be
dead tomorrow. Women, despite the fact that
nine out of ten of them go through life with a
death-bed air either of snatching the last moment
or with martyr-resignation, do not die
tomorrow—or the next day. They have to live on
to any one of many bitter ends. . . .

—Zelda Fitzgerald, from a
magazine article written at
the age of twenty-two

THE BLUE-EYED, GOLDEN-HAIRED PROTOTYPE OF THE
Flapper, who little realized what "bitter end" awaited
her when she blithely penned the above sentiments,
had been born Zelda Sayre in Montgomery, Alabama,
on July 24, 1900, the last of six children (the others as
dark as she was fair). Her father, a remote, sternly
moralistic man who was soon to become a member of
Alabama's Supreme Court, seemed scarcely to notice
her existence. Such parenting as she received came
from her dotingly permissive mother (an avid reader of

romantic novels, Mrs. Sayre named her last-born after a fictional gypsy queen and during Zelda's formative years deferred to her as if she were royalty). She breast-fed Zelda until she was four, lavishing praise on her and indulging her every whim, and soon her willful, spirited Baby—both parents were to call Zelda that throughout her life—was not only the stellar attraction of the Sayre household but a local celebrity as well.

By the time Zelda was in her mid-teens she was reknowned throughout Montgomery for her derring-do (totally fearless, she would scale the town's tallest trees, teeter her way across rooftops, water-dive from the highest perches she could find), her skills as a dancer (a promising ballet student since the age of nine, she was a frequent soloist at local recitals), and her outstanding looks ("She has the straightest nose, the most determined little chin and the bluest eyes in Montgomery," gushed the society column of a local paper. "She might dance like Pavlova if her nimble feet were not so busy keeping up with the pace a string of young but ardent admirers set up for her").

Living up to her motto of "What the hell!" Zelda soon added smoking, drinking, and necking to her list of accomplishments, and if those were not enough to arouse censure and envy there was endless gossip about wild automobile rides, nude diving exhibitions, and torrid encounters with young officers (with war raging in Europe and an army camp nearby, Montgomery was awash with soldiers). At a later time Zelda would look back ruefully on a childhood that she felt had absolved her too much from all sense of accountability and purpose, but by her senior year in high school she was as popular and sought after as a girl could be, and in July 1918, scarcely a month after graduation, Zelda Sayre, whose house was daily buzzed by admiring army pilots, who had so many beaux they had formed a fraternity in her honor, met and fell in love with Francis Scott Key Fitzgerald.

As strikingly handsome as Zelda was beautiful, the twenty-three-year-old Fitzgerald—a distant descendant of the man who had written "The Star-Spangled Banner"—was then a lieutenant in the infantry. Just weeks earlier his regiment had been transferred to nearby Camp Sheridan and when he saw Zelda perform a ballet solo at the local country club he insisted on being introduced to her. From the moment they stepped out on the dance floor together they were irresistibly drawn to one another. To the fledgling young author (Fitzgerald was then completing his first novel), Zelda seemed the very incarnation of the daringly liberated heroines he was writing about, while to Zelda, Fitzgerald with his Irish charm and Princeton background, with his beguiling stories about the glamorous East and his fiery determination to "conquer" New York, appeared the magical knight ideally equipped to transport her to a world that until now she had scarcely dared dream about.

Their courtship from the start was as stormy as it was impassioned. For all his worldly airs, Fitzgerald, the product of a strict Catholic upbringing, was shocked by Zelda's sexual "recklessness." Zelda, for her part, while flattered by the intensity of Scott's attentions, resented his possessiveness and in spite of his fits of jealousy continued to date other beaux (when at last she announced her willingness to consider marriage, it was Scott who turned standoffish, asking that Zelda wait until he had established himself sufficiently to bring her north in style).

In February 1919, Fitzgerald received his discharge and proceeded to New York, and for the next four months their romance continued by mail. Zelda had come to thrive on the Pygmalion-like interest Scott displayed toward her (when he was not reading to her he would bombard her with lists of books and cultural activities which he insisted were essential to her development), and with him gone she began to feel dull and incomplete. Her frequent letters, playful at first, soon revealed how dependent on Scott she had become in the short time she had known him. "Don't you think I was made for you?" she inquired in one of her typically all-but-unpunctuated, pencil-scrawled notes. "I want you to wear me like a watch-charm or a button hole bouquet. . . . And then when we're alone, I want to help—to know that you can't do *anything* without me."

But as the months dragged on with Scott more and more absorbed in his struggle to finish his book, Zelda, feeling spurned, began to retaliate. She gradually took up drinking again, went out riding with the "boys," and made increasingly frequent appearances at balls and parties (in one teasing letter to Scott she even invited him to accompany her to a college commencement where she intended to try her hand at "new fields"). Scott, fearful that he was losing his "princess," rushed back to Montgomery and proposed. Zelda, dismayed to see how unsure of himself Scott was when threatened with rejection, refused. The more desperately Scott begged the more adamant she grew. At last, with both of them in tears, she told Scott their engagement was over and returned his ring.

Nearly half a year elapsed before Zelda heard from Scott again. This time he wrote to tell her that his novel had been accepted for publication and to ask if he might come see her. Zelda's reply was affirmative: "I've been waiting to see you. But *I* couldn't ask you. . . . Mentally, you'll find me dreadfully deteriorated," she warned him jokingly, "but you never seemed to know when I was stupid and when I wasn't, anyway."

Lurking behind this mock accusation was Zelda's painful ambivalence about her own talents and her right to use them. "Why can't *I* write?" she inquired plaintively after she had read the completed manuscript of Scott's novel, *This Side of Paradise*. And a letter she sent Scott upon his return to New York (during his visit they had agreed that they would marry) was even more revealing. Zelda told him she had been working on a story of her own, but after a few pages had begun to despair. Her heroine was an "impossible creature," she was having great difficulty concocting a suitable male protagonist, worst of all her story had no plot, "so I thought I'd ask you how to decide what they're going to do." From seeking Scott's advice, she proceeded, within a few sentences, to give up on the project altogether. "And so you see," she concluded, "I'll never be able to do anything because I'm much too lazy to care whether it's done or not. . . . All I want is to be very young always and very irresponsible and to feel that my life is my own—to live and to be happy and to die in my own way."

On March 26, 1920, *This Side of Paradise* was published to instantaneous acclaim, and two Sundays later Zelda and Scott were married at St. Patrick's Cathedral in New York. They began their honeymoon at the Biltmore Hotel and when the management objected to their carryings-on they moved to the more tolerant Commodore. Their honeymoon consisted of a ceaseless whirl of shows and supper clubs, of shopping sprees for expensive clothes that were never worn, of cigarettes lit with five dollar bills and rides on the roofs of taxis, of champagne consumed in endless quantities around the clock to enliven their days and brighten their nights, to lull them to sleep and to soothe their hangovers on waking. A friend of Scott's, visiting them in their unkempt hotel suite a week after the wedding, was convinced the marriage would not last. Zelda struck him as a spoiled, demanding "Southern Belle." Scott was tense and irritable. Both were drinking heavily. They would, the friend predicted, be divorced within three years. After that, Scott, with luck, would write "something big," then die in a garret.

In spite of the fact that the Fitzgeralds continued to treat life as one long party, by the end of the following year Scott had somehow managed to complete his second novel—*The Beautiful and Damned*—and hardly in a garret. Zelda and he were soon ensconced in a palatial Long Island home, surrounded by a small army of servants that included a full-time nurse for their recently arrived baby girl, Frances "Scottie" Fitzgerald (shortly after Scottie's birth, Zelda tried full-time mothering for several weeks, deemed the attempt unsuccessful, and henceforth left the job to professionals—a decision she later came to regret).

As the photogenic wife of a celebrated author, Zelda now frequently had her pictures published in magazines and newspapers where with her bobbed hair she was depicted as the "Queen of the Jazz Age," outspoken, adventurous, spicily reckless, with an unquenchable zest for living. When interviewers asked her what were her main ambitions in life, Zelda said to play golf, swim, and eat peaches for breakfast. She said that while money didn't ensure happiness, the objects that money bought invariably gladdened a woman's heart. When asked what sort of work she would choose to do if she were forced to support herself, she said she would attempt to dance professionally, and if that proved unsuccessful, she would try to write.

In fact, Zelda was already writing, though under somewhat peculiar circumstances. During the past year she had published several articles under her own name. However, she had also written several short stories and although Scott's contribution to these consisted of some minor editing and revisions, the stories, when they appeared, were published under both their names, and in the case of one that was subsequently included in an anthology, under Scott's name alone. The magazines had insisted on this arrangement and Zelda gave no indication she resented it. Scott was the professional writer in the family, she the inspired amateur. With fame and fortune smiling on them as a result of Scott's recent successes, there was no need for Zelda to contemplate a career of her own—now, or very likely ever.

By the spring of 1924 the Fitzgeralds decided they were ready for a change of scene and with two-year-old Scottie they sailed for France. Caught up in the constant glare of publicity, Scott was finding it all but impossible to finish his new novel (when completed he would title it *The Great Gatsby*), and after four years of nearly ceaseless merrymaking Zelda and he had reached a point of physical and spiritual exhaustion. Following a short stay in Paris during which they bathed Scottie in a *bidet* (they mistook it for a miniature tub), they moved on to the south of France and on the Riviera rented themselves an extravagant villa overlooking the Mediterranean ("Oh, we are going to be so happy," exulted Zelda, "away from all the things that almost got us but couldn't quite").

For a while it looked as if they had found stability at last. Zelda, doing her best to stay out of Scott's way as he worked, swam and tanned herself and built castles for Scottie. But as the sun-drenched weeks slipped uneventfully by, Zelda's lifelong need for attention reasserted itself. Feeling ignored and lonely, she began to spend her afternoons in the company of a group of young French aviators who were stationed nearby. Scott, who was used to Zelda's being surrounded by male admirers, was at first amused at this latest means she had found of diverting herself, then grew furiously jealous when he learned that for several weeks Zelda had been carrying on an affair with one of her companions. In a fit of rage, he locked Zelda in her room and challenged her suitor to a fight, which the officer—younger and stronger than Scott—considerately refused. At his own request, Zelda's young aviator had himself transferred to another airfield, and a little more than a month after Zelda's "diversion" had begun, she was again spending solitary days on the beach, swimming and tanning herself as if the whole incident had never occurred.

But something had happened that Scott would later admit "could never be repaired." A chill had set in between them; a distancing, subtle though it was, that Zelda found unbearable. Before the summer was over she attempted to take her life with an overdose of sleeping pills, and while Scott, with the help of friends, succeeded in saving her from any physical damage, a psychic wound had opened up in Zelda that now gradually began to grow and fester.

Because Zelda had always been renowned for her madcap stunts and exploits, her increasingly erratic behavior at first drew little notice. Driving with Scott along a mountain road she might insist he give her a cigarette just as they came to a hairpin turn, or challenge him to a nighttime diving contest from increasingly higher perches cut into the side of a cliff. On one occasion, in response to Scott's flirting with a famous dancer, she leaped off a restaurant terrace, badly bloodying her hands and knees; on another, when Scott displayed a more than casual interest in a young movie actress, Zelda in a bizarre act of retribution (which Scott at the time merely dismissed as childish) filled a bathtub with clothes she had designed for herself and burned them. But such outbursts were sufficiently infrequent to be soon forgotten. Ironically, it was a perfectly innocent activity—one that Zelda had exhibited some skill in previously—that was to become the vehicle for her tortured spiral toward self-destruction.

In 1927, Zelda and Scott had returned to the United States. They were quarreling more than ever (Scott was finding it hard to write and was drinking accordingly), and Zelda, who had once wanted him to wear her like a charm, not only found herself increasingly barred from Scott's creative life, but to her dismay discovered that he was beginning to view her as a spoiled, self-indulgent dillettante.

In an effort to salve her pride, Zelda began to cast about for a profession that was most likely to win her instant recognition and, as a consequence, retrieve her husband's waning respect. A full-time writing career was out (Scott was too jealous of his role as the official writer in the family), and although she showed a decided aptitude for painting, her eyes tired easily and she was too vain to wear glasses. After lengthy deliberation, Zelda decided on an art form that had been her earliest love and for which as a child she had displayed an unquestionable talent and flair—ballet.

She began by taking three lessons a week and practicing at home in front of a huge mirror she had bought expressly for that purpose. She drank and smoked less now that she was studying, and for the first time since her marriage she seemed pointed toward a specific goal, but the harder she drove herself the more painfully she was confronted with the immensity of the task before her. At twenty-seven—an age at which more than a few dancers are already contemplating retirement—Zelda was attempting to enter a profession that demanded the skills and stamina of a superbly trained athlete. And she was not merely attempting to make up for two decades of lost study and transform herself into a competent dancer—nothing less than becoming a prima ballerina would do.

By the time she and Scott returned to Paris in the spring of 1929 (they were now living in France six months out of the year), Zelda was practicing as much as ten hours a day. She had lost nearly twenty pounds, was spending hardly any time with Scott and Scottie, and the more she threw herself into her work, the more moody and irritable she became (those rare parties she now attended with Scott invariably ended in tearful fights).

And still she pressed on with her studies. That July when they moved to the Riviera, she continued to take classes and appeared at local ballet programs at Nice and Cannes—the first time in her life that she had danced professionally—but as the summer progressed her manner grew increasingly peculiar. For no discernible reason she was frequently seized by fits of laughter, she began to have terrifying hallucinations (at the sight of an octopus stretching its tentacles across a movie screen one night, she hurled herself out of her theater seat shrieking "What is it? What is it?"), and at the end of the season when she and Scott were driving back to Paris, Zelda, convinced that their car had taken on "a will of its own," grabbed the wheel and attempted to drive them off a cliff.

The following spring—a decade after her marriage to Scott—Zelda signed herself into Prangins, a clinic for the treatment of mental disorders on the outskirts of Geneva. Upon her return to Paris she had at first attempted to continue her ballet classes, but her behavior had grown progressively more irrational (she began hearing voices, became convinced that her friends were plotting against her, that Scott and fellow writer Ernest Hemingway were carrying on a homosexual affair). When she entered Prangins, Zelda acknowledged for the first time that she was ill and in need of treatment, but although she had been suffering from terrible bouts of hysteria that could only be calmed with morphine and just weeks earlier had again attempted suicide, neither she nor Scott was prepared to believe that her recovery would take more than a few months.

In fact, Zelda was to remain at Prangins for well over a year, and soon she was sending letters to Scott from within its walls that cried out desperately for help ("I want to work at something, but I can't seem to get well enough to be of any use in the world. . . . *Please* help me! Every day more of me dies with this bitter and incessant beating I'm taking. . . . *Please* Please let me out now.").

But there were other letters that accused Scott of wanting to see her "humiliated and broken," and others, more disquieting still, in which she confessed she was seeing "odd things"—buildings and landscapes that wavered and vanished, people who suddenly appeared tiny or one-dimensional, their arms and legs horrendously misproportioned, their faces looking as if they were stuffed.

By fall Zelda was in the grip of what she called her "Iron Maiden"—a terrible eczema that covered her face and much of her body with running sores, and at Christmastime when eight-year-old Scottie came to visit her, she carried on incoherently, smashing the decorations of the hospital's Christmas tree. Finally during the winter of 1931 her condition began to stabilize and throughout that spring she improved so rapidly that by July she was well enough to spend two weeks away from the sanitarium with Scott and Scottie. As Zelda mended, her letters grew calmer and more objective and occasionally even displayed her old sense of humor. "We have here a kind of maniac," she informed Scott playfully. "A person of excellent character . . . [who] would like correspondence with refined young man of your description. . . . Very fond of family life. . . . Marked behind the left ear with a slight tendency to schitzopreni. [sic]" And it was not long before it was she who was exhorting Scott about their future. "Can't you possibly be just a little glad," she pleaded, "that we can be together and work and love and get some peace for all the things we've paid so much for learning? Stop looking for solace: there isn't any . . . if there were life would be a baby affair."

In September 1931, after fifteen months at Prangins, Zelda was released, and a few days later she, Scott, and Scottie sailed for the United States. After a brief stopover in New York they journeyed on to Montgomery where they decided to settle, both to keep their costs down and to allow Zelda to be near her parents. But Zelda's aging father was now seriously ill and her mother living more and more in the past, and when Scott, within weeks of their arrival, was offered a writing assignment in Hollywood, he eagerly accepted. Zelda, fearing that the loneliness brought about by Scott's absence might impair her precarious emotional balance, busied herself with the one creative outlet still available to her—writing. Working with mounting speed ("a thousand words to a gallon of coffee"), she completed a half dozen stories (one titled *A Couple of Nuts* was published the following summer), and without telling Scott—for fear he might decide she was overexerting herself—she began work on a novel.

During Scott's absence Zelda's father died, and Scott, who had never gotten along with her parents, did not attend the funeral. When he did return at Christmastime, he took Zelda, who had borne her father's death with surprising composure, on a vacation to

Florida. They spent long days on the beach that reminded them of more carefree days on the Riviera, and Zelda grew tanned and began to look rested for the first time since her illness.

Then, ominously, Zelda's eczema reappeared. It took the form of a small blotch on her neck and lasted only a few hours, but two days later the blotch was back, somewhat enlarged, and reading it as a warning signal they decided to return to Montgomery. That night, while Scott slept, an agitated Zelda took a bottle of liquor from his suitcase and drank its entire contents. At five in the morning she awoke Scott and told him that someone was "causing" her eczema and accused him of having a hand in it. When Scott had calmed her somewhat and she was more coherent, she said she felt the need to return to a hospital.

On February 12, 1932, Zelda signed herself into the Phipps Psychiatric Clinic in Baltimore. This time she rapidly adjusted to hospital life and within weeks she had resumed writing her novel (she was allowed to work on it two hours a day). Although she felt achingly lonely and despaired of ever again being completely well ("I suppose I will spend the rest of my life," she wrote Scott, "torn between the desire to master life and a feeling that it is . . . a contemptuous enemy"), her writing now increasingly absorbed her. Before long she was showing sections of her novel to her doctors, but while she told Scott that she was excited about the way the book was progressing (she had decided to name it *Save Me the Waltz* after a title she found in a record catalog) and was certain he would like it (it was, she assured him, "distinctly *École* Fitzgerald"), she asked him to be patient and not to read it until it was finished.

Writing with increasing enthusiasm and speed, Zelda completed her novel in mid-March and mailed off the promised copy to Scott, who read it in one sitting and exploded. For the past half dozen years, he complained in a furious letter he fired off to her doctors, he had been struggling to complete a novel of his own *(Tender Is the Night)*, had been repeatedly slowed in his progress by Zelda's recurrent illness, and now, behind his back, his wife was attempting to peddle a novel (without informing Scott, Zelda had sent a copy of her book to Maxwell Perkins, Scott's editor at Scribners) that was a blatant copy of the one he was writing. Actually, Zelda's novel—written in her intensely personal, impressionistic style—was uniquely her own and hardly a threat to an established author who for more than a decade had been one of the most successful writers in America. But like Scott's unfinished novel, *Save Me the Waltz* was deeply autobiographical and so touched on much the same material Scott was then struggling to transmute into fiction.

Zelda, dismayed by the intensity of Scott's reaction, wrote him a series of apologetic letters contritely offering to "submit to anything you want about the book. . . . Shall I wire Max to send it back?" and gradually Scott's anger subsided (he eventually wrote to Perkins urging him to buy Zelda's novel), but one further blow had been dealt to their already tattered marriage, and although Scott in subsequent letters to Zelda's doctors spoke of their deep, reciprocal love ("Liquor on my mouth is sweet to her; I cherish her most extravagant hallucinations"), Zelda's description of their relationship was perhaps more chillingly realistic ("We have both," Zelda had told her psychiatrist during her first confinement, "been absorbed in our love for each other and our hatred for each other").

On June 26, Zelda was discharged from Phipps. She and Scott had been arguing since the completion of her novel and she was tense and sleeping poorly, but Scott's income had dropped to less than half of what it had been the previous year (he was finding it increasingly difficult to turn out the romantically optimistic short stories which had been his financial mainstay in recent years), and although Zelda's doctors felt that she might benefit from a stay in a rest home in upstate New York, Zelda, bowing to Scott's wishes, joined him in a house he had rented for them on the outskirts of Baltimore.

In October, *Save Me the Waltz* was published. The novel was poorly received by the critics, and although only a modest 2,500 copies had been printed, it sold less than half that amount. At Scott's insistence a clause had been inserted into Zelda's contract with Scribners stipulating that one half of her royalties were to be used to pay off a $5,000 debt that Scott owed his publishers. The poor sale of the book rendered the clause meaningless; when Zelda finally received a check from Scribners, her total earnings for *Save Me the Waltz* came to $120.73.

Whatever dreams Zelda had of success and independence faded with the failure of her book. Although she continued to write (desultorily she began work on a second novel, a grim story about a heartless young woman who drives her parents insane and has them committed) and now spent much of her time painting, emotionally she withdrew ever more deeply into herself.

In the fall of 1933 Scott at last completed *Tender Is the Night* and when in January of 1934 it began to appear in serialized form, Zelda discovered that not only had he modeled the book's psychotic heroine after her, but in doing so had made extensive use of letters Zelda had written to him at the height of her illness. The effect on Zelda was devastating. In February she was readmitted to Phipps, tearfully explaining that what hurt the most was not Scott's pirating of her correspondence but that he'd made the girl so unsympathetic "and I couldn't help identifying myself with her because she had so many of my experiences."

Zelda stayed at Phipps for three months. She spent most of her time in bed under heavy sedation, and except for occasional manic outbursts (at one point she insisted she be allowed to call Scott so that he could arrange for her to travel to Europe) she was moody and self-absorbed, communicating neither with patients nor doctors. In March, Scott had her transferred to the rest home her doctors had recommended two years earlier, and the following month, while Zelda was confined there, he made arrangements for her paintings and drawings to be exhibited at a gallery in New York. Friends bought several of the works for prices that one of them described as "pitifully inexpensive," and the magazines and papers that reviewed the exhibition spoke less about the paintings than about the former glories of the "Jazz Age Priestess" who had painted them. Zelda came down to see the show accompanied by a nurse and returned to her rest home the same day. During her visit she appeared composed and relatively calm, but during the train ride back she began to cry, grew hysterical, and finally had to be sedated.

In mid-May Zelda was transferred once again, this time to the Pratt Hospital on the outskirts of Baltimore where she would remain for the next two years. Shortly after being admitted she began to hear voices, among them Scott's (he kept calling her name over and over, bemoaning the fact that he had killed her). Throughout the summer she occasionally still managed to piece together letters to Scott that movingly recalled their past ("Remember the night you gave me my birthday party and you were a young lieutenant and I was a fragrant phantom . . .?"), but by the winter of 1936 she had withdrawn completely into herself, and by spring she told her doctors that she was under the control of

God and was helping him prepare mankind for the end that was at hand. She now weighed less than a hundred pounds and dressed entirely in white. "Zelda in hell" was Scott's entry in a ledger he kept in which he recorded his and Zelda's emotional states.

In April 1936, with Zelda's condition unchanged, Scott had her transferred from Pratt to Highland Hospital in North Carolina. The doctor in charge of Highland believed that mental illness could be controlled and even cured by diet and rigorous exercise, and while Zelda remained convinced that she was a messenger of God, she gradually entered into a routine that included hiking, calisthenics, gardening, and even square dancing.

In June 1937, Scott, disastrously in debt as a result of Zelda's continuing illness, accepted an offer of six months work at M-G-M and returned to Hollywood. "Have fun," Zelda wrote him wistfully. "I envy you and everybody all over the world going and going." She herself remained at Highland. She now kept a notebook in which she entered ideas for paintings and ballets, as well as random thoughts mostly of a religious nature. Occasionally she pressed a pretty leaf between its pages. In the infrequent letters she now wrote Scott she repeatedly asked that she be allowed to go home.

Although Zelda's condition showed little improvement, she was gradually allowed to leave the hospital for short periods of time in the company of a nurse. The following June she attended Scottie's graduation from high school in Connecticut (she saw her daughter no more than once or twice a year now), and at Christmastime she traveled to Montgomery to spend the holidays with her mother. Scott, who had remained in Hollywood past the expiration of his contract, was in desperate financial straits again, and Zelda sent him a commiserating letter that recalled a happier past, "when we were first married and making holiday about the Biltmore corridors, [and] money was one of the things one simply stated the necessity for."

In April 1940, exactly four years after she had been admitted to Highland, Zelda was released. Once she had been renowned for her vivacious beauty, but now her face was haggard and deeply lined. She had long ago let her legendary bobbed hair grow out and it now reached to her shoulders. Her eyes were sadly haunted while her mouth was fixed in a permanently enigmatic smile. She was nearly forty, by her own description a "middle-aged, untrained, graduate of half-a-dozen mental institutes," and while she was glad to be free of hospitals at last, she soon found that life in Montgomery with her mother was yet another form of imprisonment. Two decades earlier she had been the most popular girl in town. Now no one visited her, she was not invited out, and she passed the long days sitting on the porch with Mrs. Sayre, taking long walks, gardening, folding bandages at the local Red Cross. Once a week she wrote to Scott thanking him for the weekly checks he sent her—fifteen dollars for pocket money, fifteen dollars to her mother to cover room and board.

In September 1940, on the eve of his birthday, Scott wrote her, "Autumn comes—I am forty-four—nothing changes." He was still in Hollywood—living with a bright, pretty English girl, Sheilah Graham, who would one day become a famous gossip columnist—and had recently begun work on his fifth novel. In November, while stepping out to buy a pack of cigarettes, he suffered a minor heart attack. At the beginning of December he wrote Zelda to tell her that his heart was mending and that if he took it easy his recovery was assured. On December 21 he was working in front of the living room fireplace, waiting for a visit from his doctor, when he suddenly stood up, grabbed for the mantel and fell to the floor. Within seconds he was dead.

It took Zelda days to accept the news. When she did she was too shaken and distraught to attend Scott's funeral (in accordance with his wishes he was buried near his parents in Rockville, Maryland). With the death of Scott, Zelda lost her principal contact with the outside world. Scottie continued to visit her occasionally, but there had never been any real closeness between them and Zelda's illness precluded the possibility of their drawing nearer at this late date.

Zelda now lived with her mother in a modest bungalow in a part of town that had seen better days. From her share of Scott's estate Zelda received an annuity that paid her fifty dollars a month (Scott's work had fallen so out of favor that Princeton University declined to purchase his papers for an asking price of less than four thousand dollars and his books, for which there was no demand, sat gathering dust in Scribners' warehouse). From time to time, young would-be authors who admired Fitzgerald's writing would call on Zelda and she would patiently answer their questions. To those who returned a second and third time she spoke of her own literary efforts and, when occasion justified, showed them some of the paintings she had done.

In August 1943, after a brief vacation with Scottie, Zelda was readmitted to Highland. Her religious fervor, relatively subdued throughout recent years, had begun to reassert itself more strongly than ever. She sent religious tracts to her and Scott's friends urging them to pray and repent. She said she would not exchange her own experience of recent years for any other because of the knowledge of God it had brought her.

Over the next four years Zelda alternated frequently between the hospital and her mother's house. Her hair was now beginning to turn gray and when she was lost in thought her lips moved involuntarily. In the fall of 1947 she became particularly weak and withdrawn and this time when she was readmitted to Highland she was given insulin treatments and assigned a room on the top floor of the main building where the insulin patients were housed.

At midnight on March 10, 1948, while Zelda was asleep in her room (she had attended a hospital dance earlier that evening), a fire broke out in the kitchen downstairs. Flames shot up the kitchen's dumbwaiter shaft and within minutes the entire building was on fire. Most of the patients on the lower floors were saved. But locked doors leading to the top floor slowed down rescue efforts and by the time the firemen had forced them open, the smoke and heat were so intense that they were driven back. It was not until the following morning that a rescue squad was able to reach the uppermost floor where Zelda and five fellow patients had been trapped by the flames. All of them were burned beyond recognition. All that remained of Zelda—almost as though the Zelda that had died so many bitter deaths over the past eighteen years had never existed—was a single charred slipper.

The ashes that were believed to be Zelda's were sent to Maryland and she was buried alongside Scott in a brief ceremony attended by her daughter and a handful of friends. At her graveside a minister recited a prayer that spoke of the painful fleetingness of human existence and Zelda's coffin was lowered into the earth. Today, Zelda Sayre Fitzgerald, the tortured, talented woman who struggled so long and so painfully to find herself, lies alongside her husband under a single headstone that identifies them as "Francis Scott Key Fitzgerald and His Wife Zelda."

JAMES FORRESTAL

OF THE NUMEROUS PHOTOGRAPHS OF JAMES VINCENT Forrestal taken during his controversial career in government, there is scarcely one that shows him smiling. Indeed, in almost all of them he appears forbiddingly grim, brow furrowed, eyes fixed in a piercing gaze over a broken nose that adds to his air of pugnaciousness, while the wide mouth is clamped so menacingly tight as to appear almost totally lipless.

With its aura of coldly unyielding combativeness, it is not a face one is likely to forget. What makes it more memorable still is the fact that it belongs to our nation's first secretary of defense, who, while commanding our military establishment at the start of the Cold War, succumbed to mental illness, committed suicide, and thus became the highest-ranking American official ever to die by his own hand.

The man who more than a quarter century after his death continues to claim this unique position in our history began life on February 15, 1892, the third son of Irish-American parents in the small upstate community of Mattewan, New York. His father, James Sr., a well-to-do building contractor, dabbled in politics, prided himself on his major's commission in the National Guard, and loved to march uniformed and bemedaled in military parades. But while in public the senior Forrestal succeeded in projecting a manly and aggressive image, in domestic matters he deferred almost totally to his sternly domineering wife. It was Mary Forrestal, a devout Catholic, who took complete charge of the education and discipline of their three sons. Under her strict tutelage the boys were forced to attend mass regularly, were kept to a rigid curfew, and were forbidden to swear or even to tell jokes. Whenever these or any other of Mrs. Forrestal's long list of rules were disobeyed, the punishments administered by her were swift and severe.

The eldest of Mary Forrestal's sons was totally devoted to her, never married, and accommodated her fondness for music by becoming an accomplished musician. Her middle son, a star athlete at school who later joined his father in the contracting business, held little interest for her and for the most part managed to escape her formidable influence. It was James, the youngest and brightest of the children, who from the start was the object of her greatest expectations, who ultimately rejected the career she had chosen for him, and who was to be tormented by feelings of guilt toward her for the rest of his life.

As a child, James Forrestal had been undersized and sickly, and because his frailness was combined with a penetrating intelligence, his mother had early decided that he was ideally suited for a life in the church. But Forrestal showed little interest in religion and, almost as though to arm himself against the overpowering force of his mother's personality, he devoted himself to body-building sports. Although it was not until his nose was broken by a sparring partner many years later that he finally achieved his long-sought appearance of toughness, by the time he was in his early teens he was running, swimming, wrestling, lifting weights, and boxing with unswerving regularity.

It had been Mrs. Forrestal's fervent wish that upon graduating from high school her last-born son enter a seminary. Instead, Forrestal became a reporter on a local newspaper, and three years later—by now all but disowned by his mother—he decided to resume his education, first at Dartmouth, then at Princeton. Determined to excel at his studies, he plunged into his school work with the fierce single-mindedness that was by now his trademark, and by his senior year had been named editor of the *Daily Princetonian* and voted by his classmates as "most likely to succeed." But in what was to prove an equally characteristic trait, he felt impelled to do battle with the school's Catholic chaplain over a series of religious issues and six weeks before graduation withdrew from Princeton rather than bow to the demands of a professor he felt had treated him unjustly.

Refusing to turn to his family for financial assistance, Forrestal took a job with a zinc manufacturing firm, worked briefly for the American Tobacco Company, and finally landed a post as a reporter with the New York *World*. Here, assigned to write stories about banking and finance, he became enthralled by Wall Street's heady mixture of money and power and, deeply impressed by the commanding forcefulness of the men who controlled the Street's activities, he decided to seek a career in the financial community.

While still at Princeton, Forrestal had been approached by a recruiting agent for a small but enterprising brokerage firm that under the name of Dillon, Read was to become, over the next few decades, one of the nation's most prosperous and powerful investment banking houses. Although the agent had urged him to join the firm immediately upon graduation, Forrestal at the time had been reluctant to commit himself. Now, twenty-four years old and aflame with Wall Street ambitions, he decided to pursue the offer and was assigned by the company to canvas the barely tapped upstate area as a bond salesman.

Attacking the assignment with a dedication bordering on the fanatic, Forrestal combined his remarkable industry with what was to prove his other most formidable asset, a genius for organization, and produced such a stunning increase in the firm's upstate revenue that he was soon empowered to hire and train additional salesmen. Within a year he had been appointed manager of Dillon, Read's Albany office, and within less than three he had been recalled to New York City and put in charge of the company's entire sales force. Scarcely past his thirtieth birthday—by now touted as the "boy wonder" by Wall Street—he was made a partner in the firm; by the time he was thirty-four he was named a vice-president; and a little more than a decade later, the board of directors of Dillon, Read picked James Forrestal, age forty-six, to head the company he had helped transform into one of the giants of the banking world.

Long before he assumed the presidency of Dillon, Read, Forrestal's association with that firm had made him a wealthy man and on a number of occasions he had attempted to use his affluence to bridge the gulf between his mother and himself. Shortly after the death of his father he had rented an elegant apartment for her in the city, and had made her a gift of an expensive fur coat. But his mother had icily rejected these and all other overtures on his part, and by the time of her death, in October 1925, had still not forgiven Forrestal for failing to fulfill her wishes.

From the start of his meteoric rise at Dillon, Read, Forrestal's friends had been convinced he would never marry. Aware of his all-consuming dedication to his work (his work schedule encompassed evenings, weekends, and virtually all holidays) and familiar with his prejudices against matrimony (wives, almost without exception, were overly aggressive and demanding; children invariably impeded one's career; most couples who attempted parenting failed dismally at the task), they paid little attention to his growing involvement with an attractive divorcee he had met during the summer following his mother's death, and were amazed when, in October 1926, Forrestal, then thirty-four, married her in an unannounced City Hall ceremony. ("I'm committing the mistake called matrimony," Forrestal informed one of his Dillon, Read associates in a note he left behind at the office on the morning of his marriage. "Unfortunate woman is Josephine Ogden. See you Monday.")

The "unfortunate woman" Forrestal had decided to take as his wife came from a prominent West Virginia family and, at the time of their initial meeting, had been a successful editor at *Vogue* magazine. She was attractive, sophisticated, popular, and witty, loved to attend parties and dances, was fond of entertaining, and was hopeful that before long her new husband would come to participate in her active and varied social life.

But although upon marrying Forrestal, Josephine Ogden devoted herself earnestly to looking after him, bore him two sons in quick succession, and did everything in her power to broaden the scope of his interests beyond his business affairs, their marriage foundered from the start. Forrestal, as if to escape what he anxiously perceived as the encroaching bondage of matrimony, soon returned to working nights and weekends. At his insistence, Josephine and he maintained separate bedrooms, spent less and less of their free time together, and before long were even taking their vacations separately. Although they were formally to remain man and wife until his death, within a few years of their marriage they were all but estranged. As for his two sons, believing that children could not be effectively communicated with until their late teens and convinced that any environment was better for a child than his own home, Forrestal had them placed in a succession of boarding schools, first in the United States and later abroad.

With his promotion to the highest post his company could offer, Forrestal soon found himself growing restive. During his rise through the ranks the combative part of his nature had come to thrive on struggle and he had achieved his greatest fulfillment in contending against seemingly insurmountable odds. It was primarily for this reason that in June 1940, just two years after having assumed command of Dillon, Read, Forrestal accepted a summons to come to Washington and serve as an administrative assistant to President Franklin Delano Roosevelt. The post paid an inconsequential ten thousand dollars a year and its precise duties were dishearteningly vague, but like the president, Forrestal was convinced that America was about to be drawn into World War II and that defeat was likely unless the public and business sectors cooperated in mobilizing the nation's resources for the conflict that lay ahead.

Forrestal found his first few months in Washington frustratingly unchallenging and unproductive and had already informed the White House that he did not plan to serve beyond the end of the year, when the creation of a new office within the Department of War prompted him into accepting a seemingly temporary job that was to alter the remainder of his life.

The position was that of undersecretary of the navy, and when Forrestal, who had served as a naval lieutenant during World War I, expressed an interest in the post, the White House quickly forwarded his nomination to Congress where it received swift approval.

Sworn in as undersecretary in August 1940, Forrestal took charge of a minor department that had been created to assist in the handling of legal matters and procurement, and with the same combination of ambition, industry, and brilliant organizing skill that had propelled him to the helm of Dillon, Read he rapidly turned his office into the navy's chief purchasing arm and in doing so established it as one of the most efficient and most powerful agencies in the entire War Department. When in April 1944 Frank Knox, the secretary of the navy under whom Forrestal had served since taking office, died of a heart attack, there was little question whom the president would nominate and the Senate approve to replace him.

Forrestal was three months past his fifty-second birthday when in early May he took the oath as the new secretary of the navy. Although he had been maintaining a punishing work schedule during the past four years, commonly putting in sixteen-hour days and seven-day weeks, he appeared remarkably energetic and fit. Among those who witnessed the ceremony there was general agreement that the new secretary, who looked ten years younger than his age and appeared to thrive under pressure, was destined for a brilliant career not only within the defense establishment but very likely in politics as well.

No one at the time realized that they were seeing Forrestal at the peak of his powers and that his confidence in his own and his country's future was about to undergo an accelerating decline that would ultimately end in madness and death. For with victory now all but assured in Europe and Asia, and the majority of Americans eagerly looking forward to peace and a return to normality, Forrestal was beginning to show the first signs of an anxious concern that over the next few years was to grow into an all-engulfing obsession.

The source of his rapidly escalating fears was the emerging military might of the Soviet Union, its expansionist designs, and the indifference of most Americans to the threats these posed. Forrestal was not alone in his fears of Soviet intentions and as the Cold War rapidly replaced the shooting one, a growing number of his countrymen came to regard his anxious warnings as prophetical. But even among those who most deeply shared his anxieties, there were few as obsessed as he by the specter of an unprepared America about to be overwhelmed by a ruthless adversary merely waiting for the most opportune time to strike.

In April 1945, President Roosevelt, who the previous year had been reelected to a fourth term, suffered a fatal stroke and was succeeded by his vice-president, Harry S. Truman. Forrestal, who had been appalled by what he saw as an ailing Roosevelt's growing inability to stand up to the Russians, was at first heartened by Truman's more militant stance, but was soon distressed to find that the new president's vulnerability to domestic pressures made him little more effective than his predecessor in dealing with the Soviets.

Convinced that he now bore the major responsibility for America's military preparedness, Forrestal began to speak out with increasing anxiety of the need for a greatly expanded defense budget and a tougher foreign policy, while privately he began to collect information about those individuals, movements, and political factions that he felt were attempting to lull the country "back to bed" in the face of the Communist threat.

In July 1947, as a result of increasing tensions between the United States and the Soviet Union, a National Security Act was signed into law by President Truman that, in addition to setting up the Central Intelligence Agency and a half dozen other watchdog groups within the government, also established a new Cabinet post to oversee the entire military establishment. Forrestal had at first been opposed to the creation of such an office, arguing that the size of the task was beyond the capacity of any single man and would result in an administrator who, having been granted enormous authority with insufficient means to exercise it effectively, would be rendered "impotent" from the start. Nevertheless, when he came to realize that the tide to unify all branches of the military had grown too powerful to resist, Forrestal took the lead in shaping what was to become the new Defense Department, and the day after the enabling legislation was signed into law, he awoke to learn that the Senate had confirmed him as the nation's first secretary of defense.

Forrestal's promotion to defense secretary made him the nation's second most powerful official after the president, and while in his letters to well-wishing friends he tried to make light of what he foresaw as the awesome demands of his new office ("I shall certainly need," he wrote to one, ". . . the combined attention of . . . the entire psychiatric profession by the end of another year") and insisted that his role as defense chief would be his "final contribution" as a public servant, his firm conviction that no one in the administration was as committed as he to the struggle against Communism made him more determined than ever to remain in government. With his political star now rapidly ascending, he was flattered by rumors that President Truman was considering him as a possible running mate and relieved when nothing came of them (like the majority of political observers, Forrestal was convinced that Truman would lose the 1948 election to his Republican opponent, Governor Thomas E. Dewey of New York, and had no desire to be forced out of office with him).

Accordingly, as the election drew near, Forrestal let it be known that should Governor Dewey be elected, he would be willing to stay on as either defense secretary or possibly even secretary of state. This announcement, combined with his failure to speak out on behalf of the Truman ticket or to contribute to its campaign fund, angered many Democrats, and when in November 1948, as the result of a stunning upset victory, Truman was returned to the White House, a number of his key aides and advisors began to call for Forrestal's dismissal.

When Forrestal, as was the custom with all Cabinet members, submitted an undated resignation shortly after the election, he was relieved to find that Truman was willing to have him continue on in office. But the demands for his ouster, rather than diminishing, were shortly taken up by a growing number of newsmen, their campaign spearheaded by Drew Pearson and Walter Winchell, a pair of highly influential news personalities, who through their nationally syndicated columns and radio programs began to take Forrestal to task for a series of alleged offenses ranging from personal cowardice (they claimed he had turned tail and run when his wife had been held up by jewel thieves years earlier) to collusion with big business (his Dillon, Read background had been responsible, they charged, for numerous policy decisions preferential to former clients and associates) to an anti-Israel stance so militant as to border on anti-Semitism.

Although a number of the points raised by these attacks were questionable if not downright spurious, the one criticizing Forrestal's attitude toward Israel had come to have increasing validity over the past year, and was reflective of a disturbing change taking place in Forrestal's personality. For while Forrestal's objection to the foundation of a Jewish state had originally been based solely on political considerations (he had feared that its formation under American auspices would result in a military alliance between the Arab states and the Soviet Union), his escalating preoccupation with the spread of Communism had by now taken on such paranoid overtones that he had come to suspect a connection between that movement and what the extremist fringe of American cold warriors referred to ominously as "international Jewry."

By the fall of 1948, Forrestal—although few as yet realized it—was already a seriously ill man. For the past year he had been suffering from intensifying bouts of depression, had been finding it increasingly difficult to eat and sleep, and was beginning to appear noticeably gaunt and haggard. Furthermore, he had of late begun to develop a series of disquieting habits: his aides noted that while working he would scratch repeatedly at the same portion of his scalp until it became raw, that he now moistened his lips continually from a finger bowl he kept on his desk, that more and more often he talked to himself.

Forrestal's associates, while made uneasy by these symptoms, interpreted them as signs of exhaustion— the consequences of an unremitting work schedule in the face of an awesomely demanding job. As for Forrestal's escalating anxieties about Soviet intentions, those might on occasion appear somewhat extreme, but they were hardly out of line with the growing anti-Communist mood of the nation. What Forrestal needed, those close to him agreed, was a vacation. Once properly rested, he would quickly return to his old disciplined self.

Meanwhile, the symptoms of Forrestal's illness continued to multiply and his condition to deteriorate. In the past renowned for his decisiveness, he now agonized over the simplest decisions, and when he did make them would brood about them for days afterward. During departmental meetings his mind would wander with increasing frequency, while at home he experienced lapses of consciousness so severe that on occasion he failed to recognize his own servants (except for his household staff, he now lived alone in his large Georgetown home, his sons grown, Josephine Forrestal rarely visiting his Washington residence). Convinced that he was being followed and that his home telephone was being tapped, Forrestal made few calls and whenever the doorbell rang would peer anxiously out of the window to see who was there. Fearing for his safety, he had recently bought himself a pistol. Now, in his darkest moments, he made out his last will and testament and started to amass a lethal collection of sleeping pills.

As the end of the year approached, Forrestal attempted to keep up appearances by forcing himself to attend official Washington's wearying round of holiday parties. To friends alarmed by the change in his manner and appearance, he conceded that he was in need of a rest and spoke of taking a vacation in the near future. But any suggestion that he think of resigning he rejected vigorously. So long as the president wished him to remain in office, he would do so.

In January 1949, rumors began to circulate around the capital that by mid-year the White House would replace Forrestal with Louis A. Johnson, a close friend of Truman's who had been his chief fund-raiser during his successful presidential campaign. But although at the request of the White House Forrestal went through the motions of briefing Johnson and even had his staff prepare background papers for Johnson to study, he was stunned when on March 1, President Truman—who by now had been fully apprised of Forrestal's deteriorating condition—summoned him to the White House and requested that he submit an immediate letter of resignation.

Forrestal was devastated by the abruptness of the order. He spent the remainder of the day secluded in his office and stayed up all night attempting to draft the requested letter. Even so, he required the assistance of several of his aides the following morning to help him complete it.

Although his letter stated that he was submitting his

resignation "effective on or about March 31," solely on the basis of "personal considerations," and stressed his continuing loyalty to the president ("I am mindful of the wish that this will not mark the end of our association, and repeat that if at any time in the future you desire to call upon me for service, I shall be at your command"), and though Truman in his return letter praised his departing secretary of defense for his near decade of distinguished government service and insisted that he accepted his resignation "reluctantly," the effect of having been dismissed from his post so shattered the last remnants of Forrestal's morale that he was barely able to stave off total collapse during his remaining weeks in office.

On March 28, tight-lipped, pale, and drawn, he joined Louis Johnson at the Pentagon for Johnson's swearing-in ceremony as his successor. Afterward, motoring to the White House for a final official visit, he was startled to find that the president had assembled not only the members of his Cabinet for the occasion, but many of the nation's highest-ranking military and government leaders. After reading a special citation commending Forrestal for his outstanding service, the president pinned the Distinguished Service Cross on the lapel of his coat. Totally flustered, Forrestal attempted to respond, but although he struggled to find the appropriate words, he was unable to speak.

The following day he was honored by the Armed Services Committee of the House of Representatives. Again there were speeches, praising him for his accomplishments as the nation's first secretary of defense, and as a sign of their appreciation the committee's members presented him with a silver bowl inscribed with their names. This time Forrestal managed a brief thank-you speech and appeared heartened by the warmth of the tributes paid him. But immediately after the ceremony, while visiting the temporary office that the Pentagon had set aside for him to allow him to deal with the flood of mail engendered by his resignation, he began to behave strangely. An aide looking in on him some time after he had entered the office found him seated stiffly at his desk, still wearing his hat and staring blankly at a wall opposite. The aide, made uneasy by Forrestal's manner, inquired if everything was all right. Forrestal quietly commended his concerned assistant for his loyalty and continued to stare at the wall.

By the time his aide got him home, Forrestal scarcely seemed to know where he was. The aide, fearing to leave him unattended, telephoned a long-time banker friend of Forrestal's, who, arriving hurriedly, found the former defense secretary in a state of intense agitation. Pacing back and forth, Forrestal confided to his friend that he considered himself a total failure and that he was contemplating suicide. He further explained that his expulsion from government was the result of a plot to "get him" that had been masterminded by Communists and Jews, and began to anxiously search the house for "them" even as he spoke.

That same evening, in an Air Force Constellation provided by the Department of Defense, Forrestal was flown to Hobe Sound, Florida, where his wife was vacationing and where several of his closest associates maintained year-round residences. Forrestal was now in the grip of a depression so severe that he could barely walk or speak. His wife and friends urged him to seek immediate psychiatric aid and after considerable prompting Forrestal agreed to meet the following day with Dr. William Menninger, the founder of the world-renowned Menninger Clinic, whom Forrestal had met while serving as secretary of the navy.

While waiting for Menninger to arrive, Forrestal, accompanied by one or more of his watchful friends, took strolls along the beach and even attempted a brief swim. But while his friends did their best to keep him under constant surveillance—even on his visits to the bathroom—by the time Dr. Menninger arrived, Forrestal had twice tried to take his own life—once by slashing his wrists, once by attempting to hang himself.

Forrestal was now convinced that the Communists were not only preparing to liquidate him for his efforts to alert the American public to their menace, but were readying an all-out attack on the United States. At moments he feared that the invasion had already begun. When Menninger arrived he held a series of lengthy conversations with Forrestal, diagnosed him as suffering from acute depression, and recommended immediate hospitalization.

The following morning, Menninger was joined by Captain George Raines, chief psychiatrist of the Naval Hospital at Bethesda, Maryland. Raines agreed that Forrestal needed to be hospitalized immediately. The question was, where? Dr. Menninger's clinic in Kansas was considered and rejected because of its association in the public's mind as a psychiatric institution. As Forrestal's friends were determined to protect him from the stigma associated with mental illness, it was decided that he be treated at Bethesda, which was a general hospital and where the true nature of his condition could be disguised from a curious public and the press.

On April 2, Forrestal, accompanied by Dr. Menninger and several of his friends, was flown to Washington. Although he was heavily sedated, the former defense secretary's agitation during the flight was extreme. Convinced his enemies were closing in and that he was about to be exterminated, he berated himself bitterly for having turned his back on Catholicism (he had rejected the priesthood; he had ceased attending church decades ago; he had married a divorced woman) and insisted that that was why he was being punished. During the ride from the airport to Bethesda, he made several attempts to hurl himself from the car in which he was being transported. As he was led into the hospital he announced ominously that he did not expect he would leave it alive.

During the next few weeks while the press and the public were assured that Forrestal had been hospitalized as a result of nothing more serious than exhaustion, Forrestal, under Dr. Raines's supervision, received subshock insulin treatments and daily psychotherapeutic sessions. Raines had diagnosed his ailment as "involutional melancholia," a term then commonly used to categorize a broad range of psychotic symptoms ranging from paranoia to self-destructive tendencies, and because during his first weeks of confinement Forrestal spoke frequently of hanging himself, he was kept under twenty-four-hour surveillance.

Toward the end of April, however, Forrestal began to show the first slight signs of improvement. Although he still experienced prolonged fits of despondency and was unable to shake the conviction that his enemies were determined to destroy him, his energy was gradually returning, he was able to focus his concentration sufficiently to read for short periods of time, and, with his appetite improving, he was slowly beginning to gain back weight.

As a result of these encouraging signs, he was allowed an increasing number of visitors (both President Truman and Defense Secretary Johnson were among those who called), and while a naval corpsman continued to be stationed nightly in a room adjoining Forrestal's sixteenth-floor suite, the around-the-clock watch over his movements was gradually relaxed.

At Raines's urging, Forrestal was encouraged to leave his suite and visit with other patients on the floor. He was also allowed access to a small pantry kitchen directly across the corridor from his suite. The kitchen's window, unlike the heavily barred windows in Forrestal's bedroom, was covered with a lightweight screen that was secured merely by a series of small hooks. Raines was aware of the possible risk this posed but considered it minor; Forrestal no longer spoke of suicide and was improving at a rate that, if it continued, would result in his being discharged within another month. Furthermore, in the days he *had* spoken of taking his life, it had always been by hanging, never by jumping from a window.

At the beginning of May, Dr. Raines, encouraged by Forrestal's continuing progress, informed Mrs. Forrestal and her older son, who had both delayed plans to leave for Europe, that they could now safely proceed with their trips (Forrestal's younger son, who at the time was working in Washington, would stay on at his father's Georgetown home). On May 14, Raines discontinued Forrestal's daily therapy sessions, and four days later, after a final interview with Forrestal, the doctor himself left to attend a psychiatric convention in Montreal.

Forrestal, for his part, continued to show slow but steady signs of improvement. He received frequent visitors, read for increasingly longer periods of time, ate large meals, and often supplemented them with snacks from the pantry kitchen. On the warm spring evening of May 21, a Saturday, he told the corpsman assigned to look after him that he planned to read late into the night and would require neither a sedative nor a sleeping pill. When the corpsman, on his way to run a brief errand, looked in on him a little before 2 A.M., Forrestal, neatly attired in dressing gown and pajamas, was busily transcribing a poem by Sophocles from an anthology of world poetry.

When he had carefully copied out the first half of the poem, Forrestal stopped, placed the sheets of paper on which he had been writing inside the anthology, and set the book on his night table. Leaving his suite, he crossed the corridor, let himself into the pantry kitchen, undid the hooks that held the window screen in place, and quietly removed it. Then, as if in bizarre fulfillment of his oft-stated prediction that he would take his life by hanging, he fastened one end of his dressing-gown sash to a radiator situated directly below the window, tied the other end around his neck, and jumped.

The weight of his body broke the sash free from the radiator and he plummeted thirteen stories, landing with a loud thud on a third-floor passageway that connected two wings of the huge hospital. When the coroner examined Forrestal's broken body shortly after two o'clock on the Sunday morning of May 22, the sash was still tied around his neck and his watch was still ticking.

Upon learning of Forrestal's death, the president immediately ordered a period of national mourning, and made his presidential airplane available to Mrs. Forrestal and her older son so that they could return from Europe in time for the funeral. Three days after he had leaped to his death, James Vincent Forrestal was buried with full military honors in Arlington Cemetery.

With Forrestal's death a heated debate began over what had caused him to take his life. His political supporters bitterly insisted that he had been hounded into his grave by Communists and their fellow travelers, the final blow dealt by the scurrilous journalists who had waged a smear campaign to drive a great patriot from office. His critics, who had deplored his increasingly strident militancy, saw his suicide as the inevitable consequence—and repudiation—of the Cold War climate he had helped to create.

Various other explanations were also advanced: Forrestal had succumbed to the pressures of office; he had been done in by the shock of his peremptory dismissal, by the unwillingness of friends to heed the warning signs of his illness, by the failure of the psychiatric profession to heal him, or, at the very least, to save him from himself.

Although Forrestal during the last two months of his life had frequently spoken of suicide both as a way of atoning for his imagined sins and as a means of ending his suffering, he had left behind no suicide note, nor is it certain that had he written one it would have clarified what caused him to arrive at his fatal decision.

However, after his death, when his hospital room was examined, the sheets of paper were discovered onto which he had transcribed a part of the poem he had been reading on that final night—a translation of the mournful chorus from the ancient Greek tragedy *Ajax*, by Sophocles. The poem's opening lines speak of a wandering son, "worn by the waste of time/Comfortless, nameless, hopeless save/In the dark prospect of a yawning grave." Describing how the son, once the pride of his race, now wanders the earth in darkness and disgrace, Sophocles suggests that it is better to die and sleep the never-waking sleep than linger on when the soul's life is gone, and in what is the poem's most stirring passage, relates how the parents will grieve when they belatedly learn of their son's suffering and death:

Woe to the mother in her close of day,
Woe to her desolate heart and temples gray,
When she shall hear
Her loved one's story whispered in her ear!
"Woe, woe!" will be the cry—

No quiet murmur like the tremulous wail
Of the lone bird, the querulous nightingale—
But shrieks that fly
Piercing, and wild, and loved, shall mourn the tale;
And she will beat her breast, and rend her hair,
Scattering the silver locks that time has left her
    there. . . .
    [And] Thou shalt weep,
Though wretched father, for thy dearest son,
Thy best beloved, by inward Furies torn,
The deepest, bitterest curse thine ancient house hath
    borne!

Forrestal never completed this final verse. When he got as far as the word *nightingale,* he laid aside his pen, proceeded to the pantry with its accessible window, and jumped.

YUKIO MISHIMA

Despite the effort he had put into the blow, the lieutenant had the impression that someone else had struck his side agonizingly with a rod of iron. For a second or so his head reeled and he had no idea what had happened. The five or six inches of naked point vanished completely into his flesh. . . .

He returned to consciousness. The blade had certainly pierced the wall of his stomach, he thought. It was difficult to breathe, his chest pounded, and in some deep distant region which he could hardly believe was part of himself, a fearful excruciating pain came welling up as if the ground had opened to disgorge a boiling stream of molten lava. . . .

So this was *seppuku!* he thought. It was as if the sky had fallen on his head and the world was reeling drunkenly. His will power and courage, which had seemed so robust before he made the incision, had now dwindled to something like a single hairlike thread of steel, and he was assailed by the uneasy feeling that he must advance along this thread, clinging to it with desperation. His clenched fist had grown moist. Looking down he saw that both his hand and the cloth about the blade were drenched in blood. His loincloth too was dyed a deep red. It struck him as incredible that, in this terrible agony, visible things could still be seen and existing things existed still. . . .

By the time the lieutenant had at last drawn the sword across to the right side of his stomach

> the blade was already cutting shallow and had
> revealed its naked tip, slippery with blood and
> fat.
>
> —From "Patriotism," a short story

THIS HARROWINGLY GRAPHIC DESCRIPTION OF
seppuku—Japan's ritual form of suicide—had been
penned by Yukio Mishima, a writer of seemingly
inexhaustible talent who by 1970, the year of his death,
had established himself as Japan's most celebrated
author. Forty-five at the time, Mishima seemed a
spectacular example of what ambition coupled with
fierce determination could accomplish. Dubbed "the
asparagus child" as a youth because of his frail, sickly
body, Mishima had by dint of fanatically disciplined
weight lifting transformed himself over the years into a
muscle man whose Atlas-like physique frequently
adorned newspapers and magazines (a Japanese ency-
clopedia used his photo to illustrate its section on body
building). Poorly coordinated by nature, he had taken
up swordsmanship, pursuing that difficult sport with
his indomitable will until he had at last become a master
swordsman. With equal perseverance, Mishima had
distinguished himself as a novelist, a playwright, a stage
director, a movie actor, and a journalist. In two and a
half spectacular decades he had produced forty novels,
eighteen plays, twenty collections of short stories, as
well as countless articles and essays. He was a political
figure, an audience-rousing public speaker, a renowned
host, and an international celebrity who could converse
and write in a half dozen languages. He had piloted a
jet, conducted a symphony orchestra, had traveled
around the world seven times, and on three separate
occasions had been nominated for the Nobel Prize.

And yet, by his own admission, this remarkably
successful man whose gusto for living seemed to know

no bounds, whose accomplishments and exploits were the envy of millions, felt his life to be all but devoid of meaning and regarded his worldly triumphs as little more than a series of masks that stood between him and the one goal he truly yearned after—a death worthy of a hero.

From his earliest years, Yukio Mishima (Kimitake Hirakoa before he adopted his famous pen name) had been fascinated by the possibilities of death as high drama. Brought up by an embittered invalid of a grandmother—a proud descendant of a famed samurai clan—young Yukio had been taken by her from his mother and kept a virtual prisoner in her sickroom until the age of twelve. Not allowed to play with other boys, let outside only in the mildest weather, Yukio spent his days ministering to his grandmother, she in turn nurturing him on a diet of tales and legends of medieval Japan. It was a storybook world of violence, pageantry, and nobly inspired suicides that the lonely Yukio hungrily absorbed, finding it infinitely more colorful and compelling than the real world around him.

A poem entitled "Catastrophe" written by Mishima on the eve of World War II when he was still in his early teens already gave testimony to what would be his lifelong view of death as a privileged romantic destiny to be savored with anticipation.

> Evening after evening
> Standing at the window I await
> An accident
> A baleful sandstorm of catastrophe
> Whirling toward me from beyond
> The night rainbow of city streets

World War II with its kamikaze pilots and suicidal battles might easily have seemed made to order for a youthful warrior seeking a fiery end. But Mishima found its stage too cluttered, too arbitrary, too crudely impersonal. Nearly thirty years would elapse before, emotionally and physically ready, he would discover the ideal setting in which to translate his fantasy into action (the war, ironically, found him still so infirm that even the conscript-starved imperial army was forced to reject him for the draft).

As wartime Japan reeled under ever more punishing blows, as its cities burned and its people braced themselves for imminent invasion, Mishima buried himself in his work, honing the skills that would soon establish him as his country's most prolifically successful author. Still, the abrupt end of hostilities in 1945—and the realization that the world had suddenly retreated from the brink of destruction—resulted in a painful emotional letdown.

> I can remember watching a movie that had been made during the war [Mishima was to write years later] and sighing at the sight of the Ginza all lit up with neon lights. But later when I found myself in a world of more neon than had ever been dreamed of, all I could think of was how easy it had been to live in a war-torn world and how painfully difficult it was to live in a world of peace.

The very postwar years that brought Mishima growing acclaim and success also left him with an increasing sense of numbness and alienation (in a world where death was no longer a way of life, Mishima could only feel estranged). Again and again he struggled to rid himself of his preoccupation with self-destruction—travel, work, weight lifting, increasingly wild forays into the world of homosexuality (his sexual preference, even though he was later to marry and father two children). Each time, however, his growing fascination with the heroic possibilities suicide offered reasserted itself more forcefully than before. Repeatedly the subject made its way into his novels; in book after book his characters talked about it, flirted with it, rhapsodized over it as the ultimate verification of existence, and with ever greater frequency carried it out.

Still, while death at one's own hands was a familiar and even honorable tradition in Japan, there were few who seriously associated Mishima with such an end. He was simply too successful, too worldly, too alive. The public considered him a colorful extrovert, a flamboyant personality who insisted on imbuing his every act and pronouncement with an aura of melodrama. Even those friends and critics who thought they knew him well viewed his frequent return to the theme of death as a form of emotional outlet, a literary catharsis, a useful protection against the act itself. What none seemed to realize, not even Yoko Sugiyama—the lovely young woman whom Mishima had married in 1958 and who would remain his close companion until his death—was that by the late 1960s, a series of events, some private, some political, had at last begun to move Mishima inexorably toward his lifelong goal.

On New Year's Day, 1967, while feverishly at work on what many would later consider his greatest achievement, the four-part epic, *The Sea of Fertility,* Mishima wrote in an article:

> It will be at least five years until I can complete this major work and by that time I will be forty-seven. In other words, by the time this work is completed I will have to resign myself to the eternal impossibility of a gorgeous heroic end. To give up

becoming a hero or to abandon my masterpiece—
the decision is drawing near and the prospect fills
me with anxiety.

I can hear people now: "But you are a writer,
and for a writer the most important thing is to
accomplish good work. You speak of becoming a
'hero'—if you complete your work successfully you
may become a literary hero."

But as far as I am concerned it is an abuse of
language to speak of a literary hero. A hero is a
concept to be found only at the opposite pole of
literature. . . . As always, the glory that draws me is
the glory of the hero, not the writer.

What had once more excited Mishima's interest in the
"glory of the hero" had been a meeting that took place a
few weeks earlier. In mid-December he had been
introduced to two young ultranationalists who wished
to enlist his aid in helping them finance a right-wing
political magazine. Mishima's young guests little realized what effect their visit had on their famous host. As
they spoke of their faith in Japan, their devotion to the
emperor, their resolve to cure the country of its ills at
no matter what cost, Mishima's childhood dream at last
found focus. Here, finally, was the opportunity he had
been seeking all his life—the chance to sacrifice himself
on behalf of a truly noble cause, a cause of historic
dimensions that would, at the same time, allow him to
hold center stage.

The timing could not have been more auspicious. In
less than three years the United States-Japan security
treaty was scheduled to come up for renewal and there
were many in Japan who believed the signing of the
pact would signal an all-out war between the Right and
the Left. As the first step in preparing for this con-
frontation, Mishima "enlisted" in the ASDF, Japan's

peacetime army, for seven weeks of grueling basic training. Though he had nothing but contempt for the ASDF's passive military posture (under the postwar constitution the army was a "self-defense force" sheared of any war potential), Mishima's motives for undertaking the training were anything but passive. He was about to transform himself into a samurai, a warrior, and what a samurai's ultimate goal was, he had no doubt. "The samurai's profession," he wrote, "is the business of death. No matter how peaceful the age in which he lives, death is the basis for all his actions."

By February 1968, Mishima was ready to carry out the next phase of his characteristically dramatic master plan. He and a student group associated with the right-wing magazine of which he was now the guiding force met in its office and signed a blood oath that bound them to rise up, sword in hand, against any threat to the fatherland or the emperor. To back up their oath, Mishima proposed the formation of a private army that would "aid" the ASDF against any aggression from the Left. This army, which Mishima immediately began to assemble, eventually grew to a size of one hundred men (Mishima—determined to totally control its destiny—limited his army to a size he could personally subsidize).

The private army's uniforms were created by a Japanese designer who had designed uniforms for General Charles de Gaulle. Intensive training sessions, under Mishima's personal supervision, took place at the ASDF boot camp at Mount Fuji. In November, at Mishima's suggestion, the cadets who had completed their military training voted a name for their small army: *Tate no Kai*—the Shield Society. Though the press derided it as Mishima's "toy army," Mishima's course was now irrevocably set. All that remained to be determined was when and how he and his Shield Society would rise up "sword in hand," a tactical decision Mishima patiently evolved over the next two years.

At first, the choice of hero's death he contemplated for himself and his followers was *kirijini*—the active form of self-sacrifice urged upon samurai warriors, a fighting death, sword in hand. Mishima envisioned the scenario for this as occurring in three acts: (1) The renewal of the United States-Japanese security treaty would provoke an attempt by the Left to overthrow the government. (2) In the chaos that ensued the police would be overwhelmed. (3) With the emperor's life threatened, the Shield Society would throw themselves into the breach, laying down their lives to protect the emperor until the army arrived. By late 1969, however, events had forced Mishima to abandon this scenario. In October a heavily armed riot force of fifteen thousand specially trained policemen had quelled a massive demonstration by the Left without any need whatever of outside assistance. *Kirijini* had been rendered inoperative. The alternative that remained was the purest form of self-sacrifice, the form Mishima had described so knowingly in his "Patriotism" story, the one that best suited his temperament: *seppuku.*

By May 1970, Mishima was ready to begin putting his revised plan into effect. To his small coterie of trusted lieutenants, he disclosed his strategy: together with troops of the ASDF they would invade the Diet (Japan's parliament) and compel it to revise the constitution, in one stroke transforming the Self-Defense Force into a proud, full-fledged army capable of waging aggressive war. As the ASDF could not be counted on to go along willingly with the initial assault, they would take its commandant prisoner and, holding him hostage, exhort the troops to join them. If they failed in this effort (and from the start Mishima was virtually certain they would fail), Mishima, as their leader, would commit *seppuku.* Masakatsu Morita, a young cadet who was his trusted second-in-command, would then behead him in true warrior fashion, himself commit *seppuku*, and—in strict accordance with the rules of this violent ritual—would in turn be beheaded by a fellow cadet named Furu-Koga. Furu-Koga and two other cadets whom Mishima had selected to accompany them on this mission—Ogawa and Chibi-Koga—would then surrender themselves, in order to be able to propagandize the Shield Society's political beliefs during the trial that was certain to follow.

On October 19, Mishima and the four young cadets who were to assist him posed somber-faced for a formal photograph in their military uniforms, Mishima's youthful lieutenants standing stiffly behind their seated leader. A month earlier, Mishima had posed for quite a different series of photographs titled "Death of a Man." The pictures had been Mishima's idea, had been staged by him, and included such graphic images as Mishima with a hatchet in his skull, Mishima ground under the wheels of a truck, Mishima drowning in mud, Mishima, hands tied above his head, arrows piercing his side, portraying one of his favorite heroes—the martyred Saint Sebastian. One final pose, ostensibly taken in jest, had Mishima seated naked on the floor with a sword buried in his abdomen, the photographer poised behind, long sword raised, waiting for the signal to behead him. At the beginning of November, Mishima mounted a photographic retrospective of himself at Tokyo's famed Tobu Department Store. It began with pictures of him as a baby and concluded some hundred photographs later with selections from the "Death of a Man" series.

By the night of November 24 all necessary preparations for the action Mishima had so carefully planned had been made. An appointment with General Masuda, commandant of the ASDF, had been arranged for the following morning. Mishima, leaving nothing to chance, had even alerted two newsmen friends, asking them to stand by for an important phone call from him early the next day. To his intelligence officer in the Shield Society, Mishima wrote a letter that contained the following request specifying what he wanted done with his corpse: "Dress my body in a Shield Society uniform, give me white gloves and a soldier's sword in my hand, and then do me the favor of taking a photograph. My family may object, but I want evidence that I died not as a literary man but as a warrior."

At 10:15 on the morning of November 25, Morita, Furu-Koga, and the other two cadets, all attired in the society's uniforms, arrived at Mishima's house in a freshly washed 1966 sedan. Mishima came out to join them carrying a sheathed Japanese long sword as well as two short swords hidden in an attaché case. Mishima, too, was in uniform. Before he entered the car he handed his fellow conspirators an envelope containing money to pay for their lawyer's fees as well as a letter in which he took full responsibility for the "incident" that was about to take place. On the way to ASDF headquarters they drove by the elementary school attended by Mishima's daughter. Mishima joked about the kind of music that would accompany their drive if this were a film. Then he began to sing, the others joining in.

As scheduled, they arrived at Commandant Masuda's office at 10:50 and were shown in. Masuda, noting Mishima's long sword, jokingly inquired if Mishima had police permission to carry such a lethal weapon. Smiling, Mishima unsheathed the sword to show it to his host and requested a handkerchief from one of his cadets with which to "clear" the weapon for presentation. At this signal, Chibi-Koga grabbed the commandant from behind, covering his mouth, and together with Furu-Koga and Ogawa gagged the general with the handkerchief and bound him to a chair.

Meanwhile, Mishima and Morita had barricaded the entrances to the office, Mishima pushing the following written demands under the main door:

1. The entire Eastern Division was to assemble in front of headquarters by noon.
2. Mishima's speech and the brief remarks by the other cadets that would follow were to be listened to in silence.
3. Members of the Shield Society that were convening nearby were to be brought to the base to hear the speeches.
4. No interference of any sort was to be attempted between 11 A.M. and ten minutes past one. Mishima would personally kill the commandant if this fourth demand was not strictly complied with.

For the first few minutes after the demands were slipped under the door there was total chaos. A dozen junior officers attempted to free General Masuda by force, only to be beaten back by Mishima and Morita, who, skillfully using the short swords they had smuggled in, wounded seven of them. Finally, at 11:35, the senior officer in charge gave in and ordered the Eastern Division to be assembled as instructed.

Eight hundred men were brought to the front of the main building, there to be greeted by an extraordinary sight. Mishima and Morita, white bands tied warrior-fashion around their foreheads, stood perched on the balcony outside the commandant's office. Billowing from the balcony were cloth banners on which were printed the Shield Society's demands exhorting the ASDF to rise up and join them in their march on the Diet.

At exactly noon, Mishima climbed up on the ledge of

the balcony and began his speech. From the first word he uttered his voice was drowned out by the angry shouts of the soldiers assembled below. Though the three cadets holding General Masuda hostage inside threatened to kill him unless silence was immediately restored and an order to that effect was issued, the assembled troops would not stop their jeering.

Mishima, who had planned to speak for thirty minutes, was forced to stop after seven. By now the sound of police helicopters roaring overhead had been added to the shouting coming from below. In the resulting din, nothing but a few scattered words of what Mishima was hoarsely trying to communicate to the assembled troops could be heard. At last, recognizing the futility of going on, Mishima signaled to Morita, who jumped up on the ledge. Together they shouted "Long live the emperor!" three times. Then both retreated into the building.

As they hurriedly moved inside, Mishima said, "I don't think they even heard me." These were his last words. He undid his jacket and sat down on the floor. As rehearsed, Morita positioned himself behind him, slightly to his left, raising the long ceremonial sword above his head. With ritual calm, Mishima picked up a short sword, grasped it with both hands, and drove it with full force into his left side. Then, much in the manner of the *seppuku* ceremony he had so prophetically set down in his "Patriotism" story, he slowly worked the blade horizontally left to right, methodically cutting through the inner wall of his abdomen.

In front of him, on the floor, a writing brush and paper had been placed in preparation for this moment. It had been Mishima's intention to write the Japanese character for *sword* by dipping the brush in his own blood. But the pain of the disembowelment was too great. Mishima slumped forward in agony and Morita swung the sword down at his neck in order to behead him. The blow failed to do the job. Stunned, Morita frantically tried again, once more failing to sever his commander's head. Unnerved, Morita yelled out, "Koga!" and Furu-Koga grabbed the long sword away from him and with one ferocious stroke completed the beheading. Morita then knelt down on the floor and, as resolutely as Mishima, drove a short sword into the left side of his abdomen. Ordering Furu-Koga to wait, he, too, worked the blade across to the right side. "Now!" he commanded when the knife had completed its journey. Once more the long sword flashed, Furu-Koga accomplishing Morita's beheading in a single stroke.

Furu-Koga and his two fellow cadets then stepped forward, righted the blood-spattered heads, bowed to them, freed the commandant, and surrendered themselves. They were crying as they were led out of his office.

The following afternoon, as a stunned nation was still struggling to absorb the shock of what had happened, Mishima's body was returned to his house. As he had requested, he was dressed in his uniform, a sword laid across his chest (for the viewing of family and friends his head had been restored). At the last moment, as the casket was about to be closed and the body taken off for cremation, Yoko, Mishima's young wife, who had first heard the news of his death on her way to a luncheon, stepped forward and quietly placed his fountain pen and some manuscript paper in the coffin beside him.

DYLAN THOMAS

Why do I coil myself always into these imbecile
grief-knots, sew myself blindfolded &
handcuffed in a sad sack, weigh it with guilt &
pigiron, & then pitch me to sea, so that time &
time again I must scrabble out & unravel in a
panic, babbling & blowing bubbles like a puny
wheezy Houdini . . .

JUST THREE MONTHS BEFORE HIS DEATH, A BE-
wildered Dylan Thomas posed these seemingly
unanswerable questions in a letter to a friend. On the
eve of his thirty-ninth birthday, Thomas's popular
image and private reality were agonizingly at odds.
With increasing frequency he was being hailed as the
greatest lyric poet writing in the English language, his
books were finding an ever-widening audience, and no
British author since Dickens had stirred such demand—nor been accorded such acclaim—for the public
readings of his works. Yet in spite of his growing fame
he had completed barely half a dozen poems in the past
four years, he was ill, depressed, his marriage was
collapsing, his drunken bouts escalating, and although
he was now almost constantly on the move, unable to
stay in any one place for more than a few weeks at a
time, he could no longer shake off his lifelong dread of
entrapment.

Dylan Thomas's childhood—though he later spoke
and wrote of it nostalgically—had been, for the most
part, cheerless and oppressive. He was born on October
27, 1914, in the small Welsh town of Swansea to an ill-
matched couple—his father a dour, pedantic school-
master who had once dreamed of being a poet, his

mother a gregarious chatterbox whose principal aim in life was the avoidance of all unpleasantness. Mrs. Thomas babied her son shamelessly; there was an older sister, Nancy, but with his angelic curls and beseeching brown eyes Dylan quickly established himself as his mother's favorite. She all but spoon-fed him until he was in his late teens and left him with a lifetime need to be looked after by women (twenty years later he was still imploring his wife to ease his hangovers by serving him sugared "treats" in bed), while at the other extreme, his father, sternly determined that Dylan distinguish himself as scholar and poet, bombarded him, from the time Dylan was in his diapers, with readings from the classics.

Simultaneously pampered and prodded, Dylan early on developed an aversion to discipline and proved a dismal student (his grades were so poor that he was unable to finish high school), but words, the sheer lovely sound of them, appealed to him from the start ("words burst upon me unencumbered by trivial or portentous association; words were their springlike selves, fresh with Eden's dew, as they flew out of the air"). So eager was Dylan to fulfill his father's dream of him as poet that at the age of twelve he succeeded in selling a poem to one of Wales's leading newspapers. His father, overjoyed, insisted on keeping the check as a proud memento of things to come. Years after the senior Thomas had died, it was discovered that his overzealous son had copied the verse line for line from a poem he had found in a popular children's magazine.

But although Dylan's determination to prove himself a poet at first embarrassingly outstripped his actual performance, his poetic voice, when it did emerge, developed with stunning rapidity. Between the ages of fifteen and nineteen he crammed a series of school notebooks with some two hundred poems (some of these already so accomplished that two decades later he thought more than a dozen of them good enough to include in the final collection of his work). When he was twenty his first book of poetry—*Eighteen Poems*—appeared, and although a few of the more sedate reviewers complained about its excessively physical imagery, overall the reception it received was glowingly enthusiastic. With the appearance of his second book—*Twenty-five Poems*—two years later, his promise was more than confirmed and soon he was not only a rising figure on the London literary scene but a colorful addition to that city's pub life.

Thomas, who to his dying day denied that he had a drinking problem, had begun frequenting pubs while still in his teens, and by the time of his first success what had begun as occasional outings had become an indispensable part of daily routine. A few drinks (in the early days beer, later whisky) would bring out the raconteur in him, and with his rich, musical voice and his unerring sense of drama he would captivate his listeners with wonderfully colorful (and for the most part shamelessly concocted) stories about his past. A few drinks more and he would grow physically boisterous, tearing off beer-bottle caps with his teeth, scampering about on all fours, barking and nipping at people's heels. Still further into his cups he could turn sullenly lewd and even combative, but at this still early point in his drinking, his companions found his carryings-on innocently entertaining.

In the spring of 1936, Thomas, not yet twenty-two, met the girl he was shortly to marry. A year his senior, blonde, blue-eyed Caitlin Macnamara was as fiery-tempered and rebellious as she was beautiful. By the time of their meeting she had been an artist's model and a chorus girl, had given dance recitals, lived abroad, and been the mistress of one of England's most famous painters. Their relationship followed a pattern that was to persist to the end—Thomas ardently pursuing her, alienating her through a variety of thoughtless acts once he had won her, then, full of promises of better things to come, pursuing her once more. "I don't want you for a day," he vowed in a letter typical of those he bombarded her with during their courtship. "A day is the length of a gnat's life: I want you for the lifetime of a big, mad animal, like an elephant. . . . I'll never let you grow wise, and . . . you shall never let me grow wise, and we'll always be young and unwise together."

In July 1937, Caitlin and he were married. A friend paid for their wedding license (insolvency, like drinking, was already a well-established habit), and for the first year they lived with his parents. The following spring they rented a small cottage in Laugharne, a poor Welsh seacoast village where they intended to live in contented poverty, Thomas planning to eke out part of what they needed to survive by writing short stories and book reviews and by borrowing the rest.

By wintertime, however, Caitlin had given birth to their first child, a boy, and soon their expenses and debts were getting out of hand. "There must be someone, somewhere in England," a beleaguered Thomas wrote plaintively to a friend, "who'd like to do a poet a good turn, someone who wouldn't miss just enough money to ensure me peace and comfort for a month or two to get on with the work I'm in the middle of now & which I so much want to finish." But no such patron could be found. Worse yet, when his third volume of poetry—*The Map of Love*—appeared that summer, it sold less than three thousand copies, and a collection of his short stories—*Portrait of the Artist as a Young Dog*—which was published the following spring did little better. Both books had received generally favorable reviews, but World War II had begun and with it the reading public's interests had shifted to issues it deemed more pressing than a young Welsh poet's evocation of his youth.

Rejected for military service because of poor health, Thomas spent the war writing scripts for documentary films (by now he had two children to support—Caitlin had given birth to a daughter in the winter of 1942). But although his script work forced him to commute constantly between Laugharne and London, and his extended separations from Caitlin drove him to seek solace in prolonged drinking bouts, he not only managed to continue writing poetry, but found himself creating with more energy and passion than at any time since the days of his adolescent notebooks.

By the end of the war, his prospects, both creative and financial, appeared the brightest they had ever been. His fourth book of poems—*Deaths and Entrances* —published in 1946, was universally acclaimed, and in addition to his movie scripts, for which he now commanded increasing amounts of money, he was in demand both as a radio writer and as a performer (a broadcast of him reading his own poetry had been so enthusiastically received that he was soon invited to read the work of other poets, to appear as a panelist, and even to act in radio dramas). Furthermore, a number of patrons were at last beginning to materialize (one of the more affluent, to his delight, offering to subsidize his entire rent).

But with growing success and stability his poetic output dwindled. He began dozens of poems and could not complete a single one. He blamed his radio "hack-work," yet when he was free to compose, he frittered away the time. From London he would write Caitlin long, loving letters deploring their separation, yet upon his return would find himself embroiled in domestic squabbles that soon made him yearn to escape. A number of theories have since been advanced to explain this waning of Thomas's creative powers: he had lost the confidence of youth; drink had sapped his energy; without adversity to spur him on he had grown apathetic. Whatever the reason, he was still sufficiently insolvent to be able to blame the bulk of his problem on his financial situation (with an income that was now fivefold what it had been only a few years earlier, he was not only still in debt and borrowing heavily, but for the first time was faced with an ominously mounting backlog of unpaid taxes).

In the spring of 1949, Thomas was invited to read his poetry in the United States. The invitation came from John Malcolm Brinnin, an American admirer and fellow poet who had recently become director of the prestigious YMHA Poetry Center in New York City. He offered Thomas five hundred dollars and air fare for a series of readings at the Y. Thomas expressed interest and wondered if a visit to the United States could be expanded to include a profitable cross-country reading tour. Brinnin, confident it could, agreed to see to the necessary arrangements, and on February 21, 1950, Dylan Thomas arrived by airplane in New York.

Thomas had calculated that the forty readings Brinnin had scheduled for him over a period of a hundred days would guarantee his return home with at least three thousand dollars. Caitlin, resentful of being left behind and convinced that her husband would squander whatever amount he earned, had opposed his going. But Thomas had been adamant. Back in Wales, he had assured her, they could live on the profits from his tour for an entire year—a year he intended to devote exclusively to the writing of poetry.

Two days after his arrival in New York, Thomas gave his first reading at the Poetry Center. While waiting to go on he suffered an attack of nerves so severe that he vomited and nearly fainted, and Brinnin foresaw disaster (an overflow crowd of nearly a thousand had assembled for the event). Once on stage, however, Thomas gave a superlative performance, using his organlike voice to maximum effect, conveying his material with such force and skill that at the end of the program he received a standing ovation.

Although he continued to suffer from stage fright and his letters to Caitlin insisted that the tour was a "nightmare," the truth was that during the first weeks at least he found it exhilarating. He was delighted not only by the enthusiastic response of his American college audiences but by the heady adulation bestowed on him by a rapidly growing contingent of female admirers. Already during his wartime trips to London, Thomas—who could not be away from Caitlin for more than a few days without experiencing a numbing sense of loneliness—had had several brief affairs. Now, with his wife a continent away, his pursuit of women grew so relentless and public that it soon became enshrined as part of his legend. It was reported that he had verified the prodigious size of a movie star's breasts by personally removing them from their bra, that he had made advances to a venerated lady novelist more than twenty years his senior, that he had chased another famous writer around her living room while her husband sat watching, that he spent his free time between readings bedding down an endless procession of professors' wives, college students, and any other devotees of his poetry that came into range.

In actuality, Thomas's conquests were considerably more modest than these stories suggested. While there was no shortage of women stirred by his dramatic readings and attracted by his growing fame, Thomas's advances, almost always attempted at the height of drunkenness, were either so grossly lewd or lurchingly inept as invariably to earn him rebuffs. Furthermore, Thomas was no longer the romantically ethereal young poet his book jackets portrayed him to be. Two decades of incessant smoking and drinking had left him with teeth that were nicotine-stained and rotted, a bulbous nose worthy of a vaudeville comic, and pallid skin that was beginning to sag. He had grown so corpulent in recent years that with rueful self-mockery he now described himself as "the poor man's Charles Laughton" (at the conclusion of his tour he told Brinnin that he had had affairs with all of three women, and even one of these later denied ever having slept with him).

By the time Thomas sailed back to England at the end of May, he was both physically and financially spent. Although he had taken in thousands of dollars more than he had originally expected, so ingrained was his habit of spending whatever money he received that, if not for the eight hundred dollars that Brinnin had secretly set aside from his earnings (and hidden inside a present he asked him to deliver to Caitlin), Thomas would have arrived home totally empty-handed.

Even so, an accumulation of bills and taxes awaited him upon his return, and the year of prosperity he had promised Caitlin during which he had vowed to stay home and write poetry was instead frittered away on endless trips to London in search of work and constant running battles with creditors. When Caitlin and he *were* together they almost invariably drank too much, and when they were drunk they almost always fought (it was not uncommon for them to wake up in each other's arms, hung over, remorseful, and bruised). Thomas spent agonizing hours trying to write in a shed that had been set aside for him at the back of the house (there were now three lively children—two boys and a girl—bustling about), but produced mostly snippets of poems, tortured efforts that petered out in mid-verse.

More and more frequently he jotted down long columns of numbers representing outstanding debts alongside his scattered lines of poetry. Among the numerous poems he planned—but never wrote—was one to be titled "Where Have the Old Words Got Me." For the most part his writing now consisted of letters to his friends. "Day after day I grow lazier and fatter and sadder and older," he reported forlornly to one of his American admirers. "I renounce my Art to make money and then make no money . . . I fall in love with undesirable, unloving, squat, taloned, moist unlovely women . . . I quarrel with Caitlin and make it up in floods of salt self-pity . . . I write poems and hide them before I can read them; and next week I shall be thirty-seven horrors old."

Less than a year after his American tour Thomas wrote to Brinnin jokingly informing him of his eagerness to be once again "imported" to the States and of his intention this time of bringing Caitlin with him: "Could you put out feelers, spin wheels, grow wings for me? I am so deadly sick of it here. I would bring great packages of new poems to read. . . . I would be much better than I was: I mean sick less often. I mean, I would so much like to come."

On January 20, 1952, Brinnin, bearing gardenias and a small square of welcoming red carpet, met the Thomases' boat as it docked in New York. In spite of having been seasick for much of the voyage, Thomas appeared in surprisingly good spirits. Caitlin, who had never been to the United States before, smoked a lot and said little. Brinnin, who had visited them in Laugharne the previous summer and witnessed several of their fights, was encouraged by the solicitous manner with which Thomas behaved toward his wife. But this newfound mood of tranquility was short-lived. Within days of their arrival, the Thomases were quarreling violently, often in public. Caitlin, convinced that the present tour would leave them as debt-ridden as the previous one, opposed it more vehemently the longer it proceeded. Envious of the attentions showered on her husband by his admirers, jealous of every woman he came in contact with, she retaliated by insulting his friends, boycotting his readings, and arguing with him incessantly. Thomas, embarrassed by Caitlin's open displays of hostility, alternated between arguing back and hiding behind his bottle. Professionally, the tour was an even greater success than the first one—word of Thomas's legendary performances onstage and off had spread across the country's campuses and he now read everywhere to packed auditoriums, his audiences greeting his appearances with a fervor usually reserved for popular singers and movie stars. But the rigors of four months of performing, coupled with constant marital strife and drinking that was excessive even by his standards, left him utterly drained by tour's end. "We were killed in action," he wrote to an English friend. "An American called Double Rye shot Caitlin to death. I was scalped by a Bourbon."

Once again he returned to Laugharne penniless. But now, in spite of his continued mishandling of money, his finances began to improve. As a result of his burgeoning reputation, his recently published *Collected Poems* was beginning to sell briskly both in England and the United States, the BBC was broadcasting his poetry with growing frequency, and mounting royalties together with fees for reprints and paperback rights were slowly but surely moving him toward solvency. But although the monetary pressures were beginning to ease, his writing block remained immovable. "I came home fearful and jangled," he wrote to his publisher, apologizing for his failure to deliver a book about America for which he had already received an advance, "there was my hut on a cliff, full of pencil and paper, things to stare at, room to breathe and feel and think. But I couldn't write a word. . . . I've lived with it a long time [the inability to write] . . . and know it horridly well, and can't explain it."

Thomas's health, already precarious, now began to deteriorate noticeably. He suffered from emphysema and asthma and coughed continuously. Frequent attacks of gastritis caused him to retch up his liquor. He occasionally passed out while drinking, and a worsening case of gout in his foot made him feel, he said, as if he were treading on his eyeballs. He refused to consult a doctor about any of these conditions.

In March 1953, desperate for a change of scene after nine long months in Laugharne, he wrote to Brinnin informing him that he was ready to undertake yet another American reading tour. Caitlin was violently opposed to the idea, his mother was against it, and this time even he had serious reservations ("I could not, naturally, leave a mother and wife and three children penniless at home while I leered and ribthumped in Liberty Land"). He had sworn to Caitlin on his life that he would keep the tour as brief as possible (six weeks) and that with the profits he would take her on a vacation to Portugal. But the trip, he was convinced, was essential; it was just the incentive he needed to get him to finish *Under Milk Wood,* a play he had been struggling to complete for several years and which Brinnin was eager to have him and a cast of professional actors premier at the Poetry Center.

In mid-April, after a series of stormy quarrels with Caitlin, Thomas set sail for his by now familiar hunting grounds and arrived in New York on April 21. His play was still unfinished, but with its first scheduled performance scarcely a week away, he began rehearsals immediately and within days found himself romantically involved with the center's attractive assistant director, Liz Reitell. When Brinnin had first introduced them to one another, Thomas had been put off by her businesslike manner while she had thought him an undisciplined boor. But by the time the two of them had seen *Milk Wood* through to its thunderously acclaimed opening (at the conclusion of the first performance Thomas and his fellow performers were brought back for fifteen curtain calls), Liz and he were inseparable. When they were not attending parties in his honor, they spent long hours roaming Greenwich Village together, stopping off frequently at the White Horse (a publike bar whose reputation soon soared because of Thomas's recurrent visits). The reading tour that followed the Poetry Center's performances of *Milk Wood* was again both successful and exhausting. By the time Thomas returned to New York in late May, his drinking had increased, his health worsened, and Liz Reitell found herself playing the role of nurse as well as lover.

A week before he was to sail home, Thomas tumbled down a flight of stairs while drunk and fractured his arm. Liz took him to her doctor, Milton Feltenstein, to have it set, and Feltenstein, taking the opportunity to treat Thomas for his gastritis and gout as well, lectured his celebrated patient on the deteriorating state of his health. Thomas promised to put himself under a physician's care immediately upon his return to England and for the remainder of his stay in New York all but ceased his consumption of liquor, but when at the beginning of June, after a tearful parting from Liz, he flew back to London, he promptly made himself ill by getting drunk at a party and left for home without consulting the promised doctor.

Back in Laugharne he tried to settle down to a daily schedule of work but with little success. He struggled over revisions of *Milk Wood,* read one of his stories on BBC television, but mostly he drank and brooded. "Isn't life awful?" he wrote to a friend. "I can't finish a poem, or begin a story, I chew my nails down to my shoulders . . . take my feet for grey walks . . . read with envy of old women who swig disinfectant by the pint." And all the while the fights with Caitlin were growing more frequent and bitter (in the midst of one particularly violent argument he smashed a plate on her head).

Even though Thomas had just recently described himself as a man who had read and lectured so often that he had grown "sated" with his own exhibitionism, when Brinnin visited him in September, Thomas asked him what he thought of his undertaking yet another stateside tour (a high-powered American lecture bureau was promising him enormous fees if he would agree to a series of readings under their auspices). Brinnin was appalled by the idea. Sensing that Thomas was desperately searching for any excuse to escape from his inability to write, and all too painfully aware of the awesome toll the previous tours had exacted, he begged Thomas to stay in Laugharne until he had rested himself back to health and could once more pursue his rightful calling—the creation of poetry. Thomas argued that the only way to subsidize the lengthy healing process Brinnin proposed was for him to accept the lecture bureau's lucrative offer. Furthermore, one of the world's greatest composers—Igor Stravinsky—had invited him to Hollywood to collaborate on a libretto for an opera, a perfect project to get him writing again. He entreated Brinnin to arrange just enough readings to cover his travel expenses and the time he was to spend in California. He would work with Stravinsky for a month, devote another month to amassing the huge fees that awaited him on the lecture circuit, then return home and dedicate himself exclusively to his poetry.

On October 19, 1953, a week short of his thirty-ninth birthday, Dylan Thomas arrived in New York for the fourth time. Liz Reitell, who had come to meet him at the airport, noticed he was overdressed and sweating profusely. He wanted a drink immediately, but the airport bar was being picketed and Liz prevailed on him to wait until they got into the city. On the drive in Thomas told her about a fellow passenger who had gotten so drunk during the flight that he had been denied further liquor and as a result had suffered an attack of delirium tremens. Although Thomas attempted to inject some comedy into his recounting of the incident, he was clearly shaken by what he had witnessed. At the hotel, he complained about the suffocating smallness of his room (characteristically late by several days, he had lost the spacious suite that had originally been set aside for him). The following morning, as Liz and he were strolling toward the Village, he spotted a billboard advertising a movie about Houdini and told Liz he had always been intrigued by the great magician, especially by his remarkable escapes. He said the worst horror he could conceive of was to be hopelessly trapped.

Over the next several days he spoke repeatedly of his own "escape" from England. Though he visited with friends and struggled to maintain an air of geniality, he was in a state of growing agitation that alternated between restlessness and exhaustion. Rehearsing his revised version of *Milk Wood*, he complained of feeling stifled by heat, then almost immediately began shivering violently. When he attempted to read with the actors, he became nauseous, vomited, and collapsed to the floor. The next morning he told a friend who visited him at his hotel that his health was totally gone:

"Since I was thirty-five I've felt myself getting harder to heal. I've been warned by doctors about me but I could never really believe them . . . or maybe I did believe it, but couldn't accept it. I think I just felt that I might be getting older faster than I expected to, older than I should be at my age."

That same afternoon, Liz Reitell took him to see Dr. Feltenstein who gave him an injection of cortisone, restated the urgency of his putting himself under a physician's care, and warned him about the potentially disastrous consequences of any further drinking. As Liz and he were leaving Feltenstein's office, Thomas was seized by a feeling of dread ("a terrible pressure—as if there were an iron band around my skull"). But even as he described the sensation the cortisone was beginning to take effect, and soon Thomas felt sufficiently better to do some shopping and even attend a rehearsal of his play.

Emboldened by this brief respite, Thomas continued his drinking. At the parties Liz and he attended during the next few days his behavior grew progressively more uncontrolled; he upset trays, spilled drinks and ashes on himself, and chased after women whether they were interested or not. After one such party Liz finally told him she no longer wanted to see him. When he called her the next day, begging her to meet him at a midtown hotel, she relented. But by the time she arrived for their rendezvous, Thomas was not only drunk again, but raving: describing wartime horrors visited upon his family that had never occurred, he ranted on wildly about blood, death, and mutilation.

Outside the hotel he made faces at passersby and cursed at the top of his voice. Later, at a bar, he told Liz he was afraid he was going mad ("there's something terribly wrong with my mind. Perhaps it's sex, perhaps I'm not normal—perhaps the analysts could find it out"). A short time later he noted a young couple necking in a nearby booth, and the poet who had written countless verses in praise of love, loudly denounced them as "filthy." As Liz was taking him back to his hotel, a young man stopped Thomas and asked him if he was the famous poet. Shaking his head, Thomas said no, he was only a clever impostor.

The next day, October 27, was his thirty-ninth birthday. He attended a party given by friends in his honor, but soon became sick and had to return to his hotel room where he threw himself on his bed, berating himself as a "filthy, undignified creature" and bemoaning the awfulness of his "wretched age." For the next few days, telling friends that he had "seen the gates of hell," he limited himself to modest amounts of beer, but by October 31 he had resumed drinking heavily again; the next morning he told Liz he had a dim memory of taking a sudden fierce dislike to a woman traveling with him in a taxi and hurling her into the street. At a party Liz and he attended later that evening he suddenly asked her if she had seen a mouse go under a door. Liz had seen nothing, but noting the anxious expression on Thomas's face, said that she had.

During the past week Thomas had consumed virtually no food. His eating habits when away from home had always at best been sporadic (on his previous visits he had frequently subsisted for days on end on a diet of Tootsie Rolls and Milky Ways). Now when food was offered him, he complained that it tasted bad and set it aside. His appearance in the last few days had undergone a shocking transformation. His lips had grown slack, his skin ghost-white, his eyes glazed, and, more disquieting still, for increasing periods of time he appeared to have trouble focusing them.

On November 3, in his hotel room, Thomas signed the lecture contract that had ostensibly been his chief reason for returning to the United States. The contract guaranteed earnings astronomically greater than any he had previously received (with the Stravinsky project indefinitely delayed, the agency was prepared to pay a thousand dollars a week for his services, starting immediately) and the signing should have been the cause for much celebration. But no sooner had his new agent left than Thomas collapsed exhausted on his bed. Only by dint of the most considerable effort was he able to drag himself to a friend's house to keep a previously agreed-to visit, and even though Liz and he stayed only briefly, by the time they returned to his hotel, Thomas was so tired he could barely speak.

He fell asleep almost immediately, but his sleep was fitful. During the next few hours he kept awaking to speak of his misery and his wish to die. He spoke longingly of his wife ("You have no idea how beautiful she is. There is an illumination about her . . . she shines"), of his love for his children ("I adore my little boy . . . I can't bear the thought that I'm not going to see him again"), but mostly of his wish to have his suffering end ("I want to go to the Garden of Eden . . . to be truly unconscious . . . I truly want to die"). When Liz assured him that he did not have to die, that there was still time for him to get well, he wept uncontrollably.

With Liz keeping vigil over him, he dozed in this agitated fashion until 2 A.M., when he suddenly sat up insisting that he must go out for a drink. Liz pleaded with him not to go but to no avail. When he returned an hour and a half later, he could barely keep his balance. "I've had eighteen straight whiskies," he announced in a slurred voice. "I think that's the record." He collapsed into Liz's lap, muttering, "I love you . . . but I'm alone," and fell into a comalike sleep.

When he awoke the next morning, he complained he

was having trouble breathing, that he must get outside right away. Liz took him for a brief walk. At his insistence, they stopped at the White Horse (where he had downed a third of his purported eighteen whiskies the previous night), but this morning he could scarcely hold down a single beer, and even it so nauseated him that they had to hurry back to the hotel. At Liz's insistence, Dr. Feltenstein was summoned and gave Thomas medication that eased his suffering sufficiently for him to sleep. By late afternoon, however, his nausea returned and he began retching violently. Again Feltenstein was summoned. This time he gave Thomas an injection of cortisone. Once more Thomas fell asleep.

In the evening he awoke to further attacks of vomiting, and as they subsided he began "seeing" things ("not animals . . . abstractions"). Liz, realizing he was in the grip of delirium tremens, urgently summoned Dr. Feltenstein once more. This time Thomas pleaded to be "put out" and the doctor complied by injecting him with the most powerful sedative at his disposal—morphine. Even after he had administered a substantial dose of the drug, Feltenstein, fearing that Thomas might prove delirious on waking, urged Liz to recruit someone to help watch over him, preferably a man. After a series of frantic phone calls, Liz located a painter friend who hurried over. When he arrived, Thomas, who was still half awake, attempted to shake hands but could barely raise his arm ("This is a hell of a way to greet a man, isn't it?"). As Liz and her friend sat by his bed, he dozed for brief periods, complaining that he still saw "the horrors" ("triangles and squares and circles"). With eyes closed, he asked Liz to describe the experience of a friend of hers who had had an attack of dt's. Liz said that her friend had seen white mice and roses. "Roses plural?" Thomas asked drowsily. "Or Rose's roses, with an apostrophe?" A short time later, as

Liz sat alongside him holding his hand, she felt it stiffen. Glancing at his face, she noted with alarm that it was beginning to turn blue.

At 2 A.M., Thursday, November 5, an unconscious Dylan Thomas was rushed by ambulance to nearby St. Vincent's Hospital. On the basis of preliminary tests, it was established that he had suffered a "severe insult to the brain" or, more plainly, alcoholic poisoning, presumably as a result of the eighteen whiskies he claimed to have drunk (there were those who later questioned the total, pointing out that if Thomas—who was renowned for his wild exaggerations—had actually consumed anywhere near that amount, he would have collapsed much sooner, and that more than likely it was the massive dose of morphine that had depressed his breathing, starved his brain of oxygen, and triggered the coma). Thomas, who had initially been taken to the emergency ward, was transferred to a private room on the hospital's third floor. Here he lay breathing heavily, an oxygen mask clamped over his mouth and nose, his eyes open but unseeing, while downstairs, friends, admirers, and the merely curious thronged the hospital's dimly lit waiting room.

Later that night, Brinnin and Liz Reitell were admitted to Thomas's room, and at the urging of his nurse attempted to speak to him. Over and over again they assured him that he was not alone, that they and other friends were there to help look after him, that Caitlin herself would soon be at his side. But although Thomas's eyes moved now and then and Brinnin at one point was convinced he heard a faint response, the doctors assured them that Thomas could not hear a thing.

On the following day, Friday, November 6, Brinnin and Liz brought in an outside doctor for consultation. His name was C. G. de Guitierrez-Mahoney, a renowned brain surgeon, who examined Thomas and confirmed the earlier diagnosis of "direct alcoholic toxicity." He explained that in cases of this nature there was, regrettably, no possibility for corrective surgery. While he refrained from offering a definitive prognosis, he pointed out that with Thomas's coma already having lasted more than forty hours, there was a very strong likelihood that it was irreversible.

By nighttime mucus had begun to obstruct Thomas's breathing and an emergency tracheotomy had to be performed. With the insertion of a tube in his throat, Thomas's breathing eased and for the next dozen hours his condition remained essentially unchanged, but by early Saturday afternoon his temperature had begun to rise and fall abruptly and within minutes the color of his face would alternate between perspiring red and icy blue. Given the depth and duration of his coma, his doctors now agreed that even if Thomas were miraculously to survive, it would almost certainly be as a brain-damaged invalid.

At 9 A.M., Sunday, November 8, Caitlin finally arrived. She had been unable to find an available airplane seat until late the previous day and now all but raced into the hospital ("Why didn't you write to me?" she demanded heatedly of Brinnin. "Is the bloody man dead or alive?"). At her husband's bedside, she shook his motionless hand and spoke to him loudly, almost harshly, urging him to respond.

When Caitlin returned that afternoon, she had had several drinks. She would not refrain from smoking in Thomas's room and disregarded the nurse's warning that in pressing against his oxygen tent she was obstructing his breathing. When she was asked to leave the room, she attacked Brinnin as well as several of the orderlies and, cursing, smashed a crucifix and splintered a statue of the Virgin. She was taken down to the emergency ward where, still cursing, she bit a doctor's hand and tore off a nun's habit before she was finally restrained and placed in a straightjacket (later that day she was transferred to a private clinic on Long Island where she was sedated and told that there was no need for further struggle because her husband was dead).

Actually, Dylan Thomas did not die until early the following afternoon, Monday, November 9. A nurse, bathing him at lunchtime, heard him utter a faint gasp, and realized a moment later that he had stopped breathing. By the time Brinnin and Liz Reitell had been summoned up from the waiting room, his oxygen tent had already been dismantled. Thomas, a sheet draped over the lower part of his body, lay motionless on his back, his eyes shut, his skin a grayish-blue. Brinnin instinctively reached out and felt his foot. It was already cold to the touch.

The postmortem established that Thomas had technically died of pneumonia (most likely contracted while in his coma), with alcoholism listed as the "principal contributing factor." His body was embalmed in New York and Caitlin accompanied it aboard the S.S. *United States* back to Laugharne where, on November 24, his funeral took place. It began at his mother's home (Thomas's father had died earlier that year), where those friends and neighbors who wished were allowed to open Thomas's coffin and view him laid out in an uncharacteristically neatly pressed suit that had been provided by his American undertaker. When it was time to remove his body to the churchyard, the front door proved too narrow for the casket and six friends bore it out through a window to the hearse waiting outside. The service at the ancient parish church of St. Martin was brief and simple. After the congregation sang "Blessed Are the Pure in Heart," the minister recited a psalm, the vicar of Laugharne read St. Paul's remarks on death, and the service concluded with the singing of "Forever with the Lord" and a closing prayer. The casket was then carried out of the church, across an old stone bridge, and up a steep hill to the grave that had been prepared for it.

Many of the poems Dylan Thomas had written during his lifetime had dealt with death and into almost every one he had injected the fervent hope that its finality could somehow be transcended: "Dead men naked they shall be one/With the man in the wind and the west moon; . . ./Though they go mad they shall be sane,/Though they sink through the sea they shall rise again;/Though lovers be lost love shall not;/And death shall have no dominion." To some degree this hopeful prophecy of his might appear to have been fulfilled. With Thomas's dramatically early passing his place in the public's mind as the great romantic poet of his generation was assured, and although he had died penniless it was not long before a flood of royalties from his books, plays, and records began to enrich his wife and children. The modest house in Laugharne where he struggled over his poems, drank too much, and fought incessantly with Caitlin has been turned into a shrine with a curator and a visitors' book. Legends about his life and death continue to proliferate, and one of the most popular American songwriter/singers of our era has paid him the ultimate tribute of adopting his first name as his own. But Dylan Thomas has not been here to partake of these glories. In a grave marked by a simple cross listing his name and date of death, he lies entombed, in the poignant words of another of his poems, "for as long as forever is."

MALCOLM X

HE WAS BORN MALCOLM LITTLE, THE FOURTH OF eight children, in Omaha, Nebraska, on May 19, 1925. His father was a six-foot-four, ebony-black Baptist preacher from Georgia, his mother a tiny West Indian woman, so light-skinned that she passed for white. Malcolm, though not quite as fair as his mother, was also light-colored, his complexion reddish-brown, his hair a coppery red.

When Malcolm was three, a local "hate society" in Lansing, Michigan, where his father had moved the family, burned down the Littles' house. When he was six, his father, an ardent black nationalist, was murdered by Lansing whites who first beat him senseless and then threw him under the wheels of a passing trolley.

With the father dead, Malcolm and his brothers and sisters were soon scattered among various foster homes, his emotionally shattered mother committed to a mental institution where she would remain for the next twenty-five years. At the age of thirteen, an unruly Malcolm was sent to a detention home and befriended by the white family who ran it. With their assistance he was enrolled in the local all-white junior high school where he quickly distinguished himself, drawing straight A's in all subjects and proving so popular with his fellow students that before long he was elected president of his class. Shortly before he was to graduate, a teacher he especially admired—a man who was always exhorting his students to fulfill themselves—asked Malcolm what he wanted to be. Malcolm said a lawyer. The teacher urged him to be "practical" and consider a manual trade instead. A legal career, he pointed out helpfully, was not a realistic goal for a "nigger," not even for one as bright as Malcolm.

Malcolm's interest in education vanished after that. As soon as he finished the eighth grade he moved to Boston, was taken in by an older half sister, and against her advice began to haunt the local poolrooms and dance halls. Before long he was wearing zoot suits, had gotten himself his own "white chick," and was "conking" his hair—an agonizing ritual that required rubbing burning lye into one's scalp in order to scorch out the hair's undesirable kinkiness.

He was still in his teens when he moved on to Harlem and rapidly graduated into "the life." Operating under the nickname of Detroit Red, he ran numbers, pimped, pushed dope (he soon acquired a habit of his own), began supplementing his income by sticking up stores, and when things got too hot in New York, returned to Boston where he involved several of his old acquaintances, among them his former girl friend, in a series of burglaries. He was a few months short of his twenty-first birthday when he was arrested while picking up a stolen gold watch he had taken to have repaired. The customary sentence in Massachusetts for a first burglary offense was two years. Malcolm's ex-girl friend was given one to five. Malcolm, punished more for his involvement with a white girl than for his actual crime, was sentenced to ten years in the state penitentiary.

In prison, six-foot-three Malcolm with his fiery red hair, flaming temper, and blasphemous tongue soon became known as Satan. In constant rebellion against all authority, he alternated between violent fits of temper and using his enormous energy to wheedle, cajole, and steal all the drugs he could get (during his first year in prison he succeeded in maintaining an almost continuous high). Hope for parole seemed nonexistent when in the second year of his imprisonment a letter from one of his brothers promising him a means of speeding his release set the stage for the cataclysmic conversion that was to totally transform Malcolm Little's life.

All of Malcolm's brothers and sisters, save one, had recently become converted to what they claimed was the "natural" religion for the black man, and when the brother who had written came to visit Malcolm, he brought remarkable tidings. God, he told Malcolm, had come to America and made himself known to a man named Elijah Muhammad. The teachings that God had imparted to his newly designated Messenger were astounding enough in themselves (God was black; great black civilizations had ruled the earth uncontested for millions of years; the deliverance of all black people was at hand), but his most awesome disclosure had been the true identity of the Evil One. The Devil, Elijah Muhammad had learned directly from the mouth of God, was none other than the White Man.

For Malcolm Little, whose self-hatred had all but destroyed him, it was a blinding revelation. In a flash he understood who it was that had killed his father, driven his mother mad, dispersed his family, and brought him to his present condition. It would take years for him to fully assimilate the elaborate teachings of Mr. Muhammad and his Nation of Islam, but that day, beholding the face of the true enemy for the first time (who but the Devil could have kept the black people in a state of such merciless oppression for so long?), he knew he had found his faith and with it his mission in life.

For the remainder of his stay in prison, Malcolm immersed himself in a study of "Black" Islam. Each day during the next four years he sent a letter to the Honorable Elijah Muhammad at his headquarters in Chicago reporting his progress and expressing his undying gratitude. Every book he read—and soon he was reading incessantly—every fact he committed to memory, became part of a tireless effort to corroborate what God had revealed to Mr. Muhammad. In his insatiable quest for knowledge he devoured everything from Greek mythology to Jung and Freud, from the early philosophers to Neitzsche and Jean-Paul Sartre. He committed huge sections of the King James Bible and Shakespeare to heart, consumed history books by the dozens, and grew so impassioned about the power of language that he made himself copy out the contents of an entire dictionary word for word.

When in the spring of 1952 Malcolm was paroled (three years had been deducted from his sentence for good behavior), he joined his brothers and sisters then living in Detroit and immediately applied for membership in the Nation of Islam. As soon as he could arrange it, he traveled to Chicago to hear Elijah Muhammad speak and discovered that the impact of seeing the Messenger in person was even greater than the revelation he had received while in prison. The man who had been personally instructed by God entered Chicago's Mosque Number 2 (the mosques were numbered in the order in which they had been established) surrounded by a retinue of towering, grim-faced young men. By contrast, Elijah Muhammad was tiny. His face was small and gentle-looking. He wore a dark suit, a red bow tie, and a gold-embroidered fez. When he spoke his voice was barely audible, yet no one in the auditorium missed a single word he said. Mr. Muhammad told of how he had devoted his life to preaching Allah's word. He noted sadly that the majority of blacks in America were ignorant of God's wisdom and were therefore morally and spiritually dead. He explained that the black man was the Original Man and that with self-knowledge he would lift himself back to his rightful place at the top of civilization. And then he called out Malcolm's name and asked him to stand.

Introducing a dazed Malcolm to the congregation, Mr. Muhammad spoke fondly of their correspondence, of how "strong" Malcolm had become in prison, of how certain he was that Malcolm would remain forever faithful to Islam. And as if that were not praise enough, he invited his overwhelmed young visitor to dine with him at his home that very evening.

Shortly after Malcolm returned to Detroit, his application for membership in the Nation was accepted and he was presented with his X. According to the Muslims, the X symbolizes the African family name that no American black will ever know. ("Mr. Muhammad," Malcolm wrote later, "taught that we would keep this X until God himself returned and gave us a Holy Name from His own mouth"). Imbued with a convert's zeal, Malcolm threw himself into the task of recruiting new members for the Detroit mosque. So successful were his efforts that within months he was named the mosque's assistant minister. The following year, promoted to full minister at the behest of Mr. Muhammad, he founded new temples in Boston and Philadelphia, and in April 1954, as a reward for his outstanding work on behalf of the Nation, the Messenger granted to Malcolm X, not yet twenty-nine, the pastorate second in importance only to his own—the ministry of Mosque Number 7, in Harlem.

Mosque Number 7, at the time Malcolm took it over, was a storefront in the poorest section of the ghetto (in 1954 the total Muslim membership nationwide numbered less than a thousand), and at first Malcolm's evangelical zeal met with considerable resistance. It took him three years to build his congregation from a few dozen to a few hundred members, and to recruit that number he had to scour the back streets and poolrooms and even poach off the local churches. And then, in the spring of 1957, just when it seemed that all possible avenues to enlarge his ministry had been exhausted, a Muslim named Hinton Johnson got beaten up by the police one evening, and before the night was over, Malcolm X had become a power in Harlem.

The brutalizing of blacks by police was then an everyday occurence in the ghettos of America. What made the Hinton Johnson incident different was that Johnson belonged to the Nation of Islam, and when Malcolm learned of the beating he marched his people to the local precinct where Johnson was being held. It was not Malcolm's intention to incite them to riot (the Muslim religion forbids acts of violence except in self-defense), but it was clear he would not order them to disperse until he was satisfied that Brother Hinton was being properly treated.

Neither the police nor the people of Harlem had ever seen a demonstration quite like the one that night. Across the street from the precinct, arms folded, as motionless as statues, stood the men of Mosque Number 7. Behind them, equally impassive, stood their women in ankle-length white dresses and scarves. All had their eyes fixed on the police station, and with every passing minute the crowd behind the Muslims kept growing until it numbered in the thousands.

At two in the morning the police finally asked to see Malcolm. It was unprecedented for police officials to negotiate with a black man and at first they refused to acknowledge that they required his assistance. It was only when Malcolm threatened to walk out that they bowed to his terms, allowed him to visit with Johnson, and when Malcolm demanded that the battered Muslim be transferred to a hospital (Johnson later sued the city and was awarded seventy thousand dollars), they promptly acceded to his request. Malcolm, in turn, satisfied that Muslim rights had been respected, stepped into the street, signaled his people to disperse, and without so much as a word his mute legions dissolved into the night.

After that everyone in Harlem knew who Malcolm X was. Membership in Mosque Number 7 swelled rapidly, wherever Malcolm went people sought out his opinions and advice, and Harlem's largest newspaper, the *Amsterdam News,* invited him to write a weekly column. Before long it was Malcolm who was being written about in newspapers and magazines (reporters found him scary, fascinating, and—most important—excellent copy). Soon he was not only a popular figure on television news shows but a star of the university lecture circuit (his sardonic humor and slashing style made him one of the most sought-after speakers on America's campuses), and within a year of the Hinton Johnson affair, Malcolm X and the Black Muslims (a black sociologist had dubbed them that) had become household words throughout the land.

As his fame grew, Malcolm labored ever more mightily on behalf of the Nation, taking the White Devil to task at every turn. Unlike the integrationists whose dream was a color-blind America, Malcolm, preaching Muslim dogma, thought it no boon for blacks to participate in what was clearly a racist society ("Whenever I refer to America," he would tell white audiences, "I don't say *we.* I don't say *I* or *our.* I say *you . . . your* president, *your* Congress, *your* Senate, and *your* troubles"). He was cynical about this country's leaders, even those most respected for their good intentions; refused to believe that blacks would ever be accepted by the majority of Americans; preached the separation of the races (either a return to the "East" or a separate "black state" within this country's national boundaries); insisted on black people's right to self-defense; and scoffed at the turn-the-other-cheek forbearance of most civil rights leaders ("Martin Luther King isn't preaching love," he observed disdainfully, "he's preaching love the white man").

Still, it was King who had filled the streets of Birmingham with protesting demonstrators; who had succeeded in pressuring the president and Congress into enacting a civil rights law; who had led the great march on Washington and stirred it with his rhetoric. As the civil rights movement of the early 1960s grew in scope and intensity, as police dogs were unleashed on peaceful marchers, as black churches were bombed, young freedom fighters lynched, and innocent black children murdered, Malcolm, feeling more and more hemmed in by the Allah-will-decide-when-to-deal-with-the-Devil philosophy of Mr. Muhammad, petitioned Chicago to allow him to join in the struggle. Chicago turned him down. If his cadres could not demonstrate, might they not at least be allowed to protect those who did? Again his request was denied. In the spring of 1962, a shoot-out initiated by the Los Angeles police left one Muslim dead and a half dozen seriously wounded. Malcolm, who had personally organized the Los Angeles mosque and knew most of the victims, requested permission to retaliate. The Messenger refused to grant it and this time Malcolm wept with frustration and shame.

Although Malcolm, as he always had in the past, complied with the wishes of his mentor, a rift was gradually beginning to develop between the two men. For a dozen years they had been like father and son, Elijah Muhammad showering ever-greater honors on the most promising of his disciples, Malcolm devotedly—some thought obsequiously—deferring to the man through whom he had found his salvation ("I am not the author of anything I say," he insisted repeatedly. "I am just a little Charlie McCarthy who's sitting on the Messenger's knee").

But as Malcolm's political consciousness grew, he found the role of puppet increasingly difficult to sustain. And as his restiveness increased, slowly, reluctantly, Malcolm began to perceive that his Godlike savior, the exalted author of his resurrection, possessed the flaws of an all-too-mortal man.

For some time Malcolm had been hearing rumors about Mr. Muhammad's private life. There had been stories that a number of the Messenger's secretaries had become pregnant while in his service. To Malcolm, for whom Elijah Muhammad was a symbol of moral perfection (so influenced had Malcolm been by his example that from the time he entered prison until he married twelve years later he had not touched a woman), the mere notion that it was perhaps the Messenger who had impregnated the secretaries was unthinkable. Now, as the rumors multiplied, Malcolm could ignore them no longer. He wrote to Elijah Muhammad informing him about the stories that were being spread about him. The Messenger telephoned Malcolm in New York and invited him to fly to his winter retreat in Phoenix where they could discuss the matter in person.

As always when greeting one another they embraced warmly and then began to walk around Mr. Muhammad's swimming pool. In a faltering voice, Malcolm repeated the rumors he had heard (at any moment he expected the Messenger to angrily stop him and refute them) and was astonished when the old man nodded instead, explaining that what Malcolm had heard was a fulfillment of Biblical prophecy. "I am David," Malcolm quoted him as saying later. "When you read about how David took another man's wife, I'm that David. You read about Noah, who got drunk—that's me. You read about Lot, who went and laid up with his own daughters. I have to fulfill all those things."

Malcolm was devastated. The man he had believed to be divinely guided was not only a philanderer but a hypocrite. Nevertheless, Malcolm felt it essential that the Nation be protected should the scandal break, and upon his return to New York he convened a meeting of the East Coast Muslim leaders to acquaint them with the facts. It was a disastrous blunder on his part. Malcolm had always been dangerously oblivious of the jealousies and resentments his favorite-son status provoked among his fellow ministers. Now, instead of accepting Malcolm's confidences in the constructive spirit in which they were offered, a number of the ministers sent reports to Elijah Muhammad accusing Malcolm of spreading false rumors about the Messenger with the intent of dethroning him.

Although there was no immediate response from Chicago, retribution was not long in coming. On November 22, 1963, President John F. Kennedy was assassinated in Dallas, and a few days later Elijah Muhammad, who was to be the main speaker at a Muslim rally in New York, canceled his appearance and, as he had frequently done in the past, asked Malcolm to go on in his place.

Complying, Malcolm delivered one of his routine speeches—"God's Judgment of White America"—and during the question-and-answer period that followed was asked how he felt about the presidential assassination. Malcolm said he thought it a logical consequence of white America's violence toward blacks spreading unchecked until it had finally struck down its own chief of state. It was, he said, "a case of the chickens coming home to roost."

The next morning the remark made headlines

throughout the country, and before the day was out Malcolm received a telephone call from Mr. Muhammad ordering him to Chicago. This time the Messenger's embrace lacked its usual "amiability." He asked Malcolm if he had seen the newspapers ("That was a very bad statement," he told Malcolm in a mild but chilling voice. "That was very ill timed. I'll have to silence you for the next ninety days so that Muslims everywhere can be dissociated from the blunder").

Malcolm did his best to accept his punishment stoically ("I disobeyed Mr. Muhammad," he told reporters upon his return to New York. "I submit completely to his wisdom.") But he soon learned that his "silencing" was to be more severe than had been originally suggested. Chicago informed him that he was not only forbidden to speak to the press but banned from preaching in his own mosque. Next he was told that he would be reinstated only if he "submitted" totally to Mr. Muhammad's will. When he protested that he had already done so, he was summoned to a secret hearing and found himself confronted not only by a wrathful Messenger but by several highly placed Muslims who were known for their antagonism toward him. During the stormy meeting that followed—in the course of which Mr. Muhammad accused his most devoted follower of treachery—Malcolm pleaded for and was granted permission to defend himself before the members of his own mosque, but upon his return to Harlem he learned that word had been sent down from headquarters ordering him "isolated." Until such a time as the Messenger lifted this most stringent of quarantines, all men and women belonging to the Nation were forbidden to communicate with Malcolm in any manner whatsoever.

In the terminology of Black Islam the world outside the mosque is referred to as the grave and those forced to inhabit it as the dead. Malcolm was still very much alive (although so shaken by what had occurred that he insisted on a brain examination to ensure himself that his mind was intact), but the man he had loved more than his own father had repudiated him, the Nation in which he had served unstintingly for a dozen years was casting him out, and as if that were not enough, Malcolm soon perceived that among his recent brethren there were those who yearned for more than just his symbolic demise.

Nevertheless, he waited until the ninety days had expired, attempted one last time by letter and telephone to affect a reconciliation, and then, accepting the painful truth at last—that reconciliation would never come—he called a press conference and announced the formation of his own organization—Muslim Mosque, Incorporated.

It was only now that Malcolm began to realize how isolated he had become. Barred from the Kingdom of Heaven (for had not Allah entrusted his Messenger with the sole set of keys to its gate?), he found himself equally spurned by those civil rights leaders to whom he now made belated overtures (they considered him too extreme, too unpredictable, and, though few would admit it, too threatening a rival). And although reporters flocked to him each time he had a new announcement to make (among the numerous projects he proposed in the first hectic weeks were organizing a drug-addict program for Harlem, starting up his own newspaper, and convening a black nationalist convention), the truth was that after a decade of virtually unlimited power, Malcolm was broke, adrift, his new ministry confined to a single Harlem hotel room, his once vast constituency reduced to a handful of uneasy adherents (of the more than two thousand members

Malcolm had brought into Mosque Number 7, less than fifty had followed him when he left).

And before long even his most loyal supporters found themselves questioning their judgment. For in April 1964, Malcolm, announcing that he was eager to learn the ways of "true Islam," undertook a pilgrimage to Mecca in Saudi Arabia and soon discovered that in one critical respect the Muslims of the East followed a faith very different from the one preached by Elijah Muhammad: among the original followers of the Koran, race played no part whatsoever. Malcolm was stunned. For days his mind struggled against what his eyes were telling him, but everywhere he looked the message was reiterated. "They were of all colors, from blue-eyed blonds to black-skinned Africans," he wrote of his fellow pilgrims in a letter he sent home for distribution to the press. "But we were all participating in the same ritual, displaying a spirit of unity and brotherhood that my experiences in America had led me to believe never could exist between the white and the non-white. . . . You may be shocked by these words coming from me. But on this pilgrimage, what I have seen, and experienced, has forced me to *re-arrange* much of my thought-patterns previously held."

His "re-arrangement" did not absolve the racist ways of "Christian" white America (during the tour of Africa he undertook immediately following his pilgrimage he urged the leaders of that continent to sponsor a United Nations resolution condemning the oppression of blacks in the United States), but when he returned to New York in mid-May, wispy-bearded and sporting an astrakhan hat, he was no longer simply Malcolm X, but El-Hajj Malik El-Shabazz, a Sunni Muslim, a prophet in the midst of reshaping himself, and all too dangerously alone in a homeland that was fast becoming enemy territory.

The first attack—the Muslims launched it almost immediately upon his return—was directed not at his person but at his house. In 1957, three years after Elijah Muhammad had appointed him minister of Mosque Number 7, Malcolm, deciding the time had come for him to take a wife, had begun a cautious courtship of a member of his Harlem congregation. Her mosque name was Sister Betty X. A strikingly handsome, strong-willed young woman (she had become a Muslim in spite of her foster parents' threat to disown her), Sister Betty was highly intelligent, college-educated—practical—to support herself she had become a registered nurse—and at nearly six feet, as Malcolm used to point out jokingly, "the right height for somebody my height."

They had married in January 1958 and for the first two and a half years they lived in a small house in Queens which they shared with another Muslim couple. By that time Betty had given birth to two of their four daughters, and Elijah Muhammad, eager to reward the most dedicated and gifted of all his ministers, had presented him with his own house in East Elmhurst, Queens. As houses went it was not much—a modest brick structure assessed at just over sixteen thousand dollars. But, aside from his car, it was the only physical asset Malcolm had to show for twelve years of tireless labor on behalf of the Nation, and now the Muslims informed him they wanted it back. The eviction suit was tried in Queens Civil Court, Malcolm swearing Elijah Muhammad had deeded him the house outright as a reward for his labors, the Muslims (who held the actual deed) insisting it was a ministry home, with Malcolm entitled to use it only so long as he held the post.

In the three months since Malcolm had quit the

Nation, he had done his utmost to play down any personal animosity between Elijah Muhammad and himself ("You are still my teacher and leader," he had wired the Messenger shortly after the formation of his own mosque). But with his family threatened with eviction, with Muslim troops beginning to shadow him wherever he went, with the attacks against him in Mr. Muhammad's newspaper growing daily more vindictive ("If it were not for the Messenger," read a typical attack, "you would still be just another unheard-of penny-ante Harlem hustler"), Malcolm could wave the olive branch no longer. Taking the witness stand on the last day of his trial, he blurted out the real reason for his suspension from the Nation: it had nothing to do, he said, with his remark about President Kennedy; the sole reason he was being persecuted was his disclosure to fellow ministers of what he had learned about the sexual improprieties of Elijah Muhammad.

When Malcolm returned home that evening, he found that his telephone had gone dead (a woman identifying herself as "Mrs. Small"—a cruel play on his slave name, Little—had called the phone company requesting that Malcolm's telephone be disconnected while he was away on "vacation"). Later that night a brawl between a group of Muslims and a handful of his followers had to be broken up by the police. And although the Messenger in his newspaper *Muhammad Speaks* insisted that "hypocrites" like Malcolm were not to be killed because "Allah desires to make them examples for others by chastising them like a parent does a child," before long Harlem was aflame with rumors of Malcolm's imminent assassination by agents of the Nation. "There is no group in the United States more able to carry out this threat than the Black Muslims," Malcolm concurred grimly. "I know because I taught them myself."

In July 1964 Malcolm left on his second trip to Africa. He was enthusiastically received everywhere he went; students especially were stirred by his passionate insistence that a link be established between the blacks of Africa and those of the United States. But in his continuing effort to push forward a UN resolution condemning racism, he found himself isolated from Africa's moderate leaders just as his increasingly ecumenical attitude toward whites was alienating him from his followers back home. In Ghana, the last stop on his tour, his friends, noting the stress he was under, entreated him to send for Betty and the children and stay until things cooled off in the United States. Malcolm was moved by their concern, but declined. It was not, he explained, that he was brave or foolhardy or unaware of the dangers that awaited him in America. It was just simply that that was where he belonged.

When he returned to New York in November, he found his organization in total disarray. A number of his more conservative followers had defected, the mosque's coffers were empty, and in an effort to replenish them Malcolm accepted speaking engagements across the country that soon left him without a moment's rest (his punishing schedule rarely allowed him more than four hours of sleep a night). Everywhere he traveled now he encountered Muslims, their ominously expressionless faces greeting him at airport terminals, in the auditoriums where he spoke, even in the lobbies of the hotels where he stayed. Soon he had himself photographed in his home holding an automatic rifle that he had procured against possible assassination attempts (he had taught his wife to use it as well, he explained to the press, instructing her to fire on anyone who tried to force his way inside their home).

"You are now the target of your own followers, which are very few, *and* the followers of Muhammad," the

Nation's newspaper warned ominously. And in January 1965, when Malcolm traveled to Los Angeles to meet with the secretaries who were filing paternity suits against the Messenger (their suits were later dropped), two carloads of Muslims pursued him as he was returning to the airport and were warded off only when Malcolm suddenly grabbed a cane and thrust it out his car window as if it were a rifle.

On Sunday, February 14, 1965, Malcolm was in New York, asleep with his family in their East Elmhurst home, when at three o'clock in the morning two Molotov cocktails exploded through the picture window of his living room, setting the house on fire. Scooping up his screaming children from their beds, he got them and his pregnant wife out of the house into the subfreezing cold, then raced back in to rescue what clothes and belongings he could (it took the fire department an hour to put out the flames, and by the time they did half the uninsured house was gone).

As soon as Malcolm had settled Betty and his four daughters in the house of a friend, he flew to Detroit where he was scheduled to speak that afternoon. He had always made it a point to keep his speaking dates, but this time when he climbed to the podium his clothes were scorched and rumpled and he meandered through his speech, too stunned and angry to be able to keep his mind on what he was saying (in New York the Muslims had called a press conference that morning and accused Malcolm of having fire-bombed his own house in an effort to gain publicity!).

The week that followed was a growing nightmare. On his return to New York Malcolm learned that the court had ordered him evicted from his home, and he was forced to steal into his house in the middle of the night to remove what remained of his family's belongings. He called a press conference at which he warned that the

Muslims were determined to kill him, attacked the police for their indifference, and demanded an investigation by the FBI. He applied for a permit to carry a handgun and made an appointment with his lawyer for the following week to draw up a will. "I did many things as a Muslim that I'm sorry for now," he told an interviewer from *Life* magazine. "That was a bad scene, brother. The sickness and madness of those days—I'm glad to be free of them." When the interviewer asked why he did not demand greater protection, Malcolm, laughing bitterly, replied, "Brother, nobody can protect you from a Muslim *but* a Muslim."

On the following Saturday, February 20, Malcolm drove out with Betty and a real estate agent to look at houses (when they found one they liked, he told her he would ask for an additional advance on the autobiography he was writing to cover the down payment). Afterward, as he was driving Betty to a friend's home where she and the children were temporarily staying, Malcolm apologized for the long separations he had subjected her to and promised he would never leave her again (unbeknown to Betty he had already written to associates in Africa asking them to take in Betty and his four daughters should anything happen to him).

Late that afternoon, after a tense policy meeting with his key followers at which Malcolm complained about how little they were getting done, he drove to the Hilton Hotel in midtown Manhattan and checked into a twelfth-floor room where he slept undisturbed for the first time in days. At exactly eight o'clock the next morning the telephone alongside his bed rang, awakening him. Malcolm, desperate for a few hours of quiet, had purposely told no one of his whereabouts, but when he picked up the receiver, a man's voice said "Wake up, brother" and hung up.

Malcolm had scheduled a Harlem rally for two

o'clock that afternoon. He had told Betty he did not want her to come, but toward noon he called her to say that he had changed his mind and asked her to bring the children. Then, as the time of the rally neared, Malcolm donned his familiar minister's garb (dark suit, white shirt, black tie), checked out of the hotel, retrieved his car from its garage, and slowly drove uptown.

Since his ouster from the Nation, Malcolm had been holding frequent Sunday rallies at the Audubon Ballroom in Washington Heights. At the start the crowds had jammed the auditorium to overflowing, but as Malcolm's fiery oratory had moderated, the crowds had gradually dwindled, and with still others frightened off by the growing threats of the Muslims, the hall was less than a quarter full when Malcolm arrived shortly before 2 P.M.

Usually there were at least a half dozen police officers stationed directly outside the building, but on this unusually balmy February afternoon there was just one (the police would later claim that at the request of one of Malcolm's own aides, who was never identified, the bulk of the twenty-man security force assigned to protect Malcolm had been hidden away inside Columbia Presbyterian Medical Center, a hospital directly across the street). If Malcolm noticed the absence of police, he did not comment on it. Although he had been complaining bitterly to the press for weeks about insufficient police protection, he had adamantly forbidden their presence inside the ballroom, and today he was so preoccupied that he seemed scarcely conscious of his whereabouts.

Looking drawn and haggard, he proceeded inside, crossed the ballroom, and retired to a small dressing room adjoining the stage where, along with several of his assistants, he waited for the guest speakers he had invited to arrive. By half past two, when none of them had shown up, Malcolm asked Benjamin X, one of his closest associates, to go out and deliver the warm-up speech and stretch it out as long as possible. Thirty minutes later there were still no guest speakers on the platform and Benjamin X had no recourse but to introduce Malcolm ("And now without further remarks, I present to you one who is willing to put himself on the line for you, a man who would give his life for you"). Malcolm rose and entered the auditorium. While waiting in the dressing room he had been increasingly tense and irritable, pacing back and forth, snapping at his lieutenants, brusquely dismissing their complaints about lax security on the floor. Now, as Malcolm walked out onto the stage, the fervent applause from the small but dedicated audience visibly buoyed him up and by the time he reached the podium he was smiling for the first time in days.

"As-salaam-alaikum, brothers and sisters!" Malcolm called out (they were the words with which he opened every meeting—the Arabic for "Peace be unto you"), and those present who were his followers responded with *"Wa-alaikum salaam!"* ("And unto you be peace"). No sooner had these greetings been exchanged than a scuffle erupted near the back of the room, two black men shoving one another, one of them angrily demanding "What you doing in my pocket? Get your hands out of my pocket!" Heads in the audience swiveled anxiously. Malcolm's bodyguards moved forward from their posts in front of the stage to deal with the disturbance. "Hold it! Hold it!" Malcolm pleaded, trying to calm both the combatants and the audience. "Let's cool it! Let's be cool, brothers!"

Even as he called out these words, a black man near the front of the room jumped to his feet, whipped a sawed-off shotgun from underneath his coat, and fired. The report was deafening. A dozen buckshot pellets tore through the lectern behind which Malcolm stood and drilled a perfect circle—seven inches in diameter— in the center of his chest. Malcolm's hands flew instinctively to the wound. For a moment Malcolm remained on his feet, a dark stain spreading across his white shirt. Then, his eyes rolling up in his head, he toppled backward, treelike, knocking over several of the folding chairs reserved for the guest speakers who had never arrived. As Malcolm's head crashed to the floor, the man with the shotgun fired a second time and now two more black men at the front of the ballroom were on their feet, firing pistols at Malcolm's twitching body as well.

By the time Betty was able to fight her way through to the stage (at the sound of the shots she had thrown herself over her shrieking children), Malcolm's face was ashen, his mouth distended in a terrible, teeth-bared grin. Someone had pulled open his blood-stained shirt and a crying woman was trying to give him mouth-to-mouth resuscitation, but one glance told Betty, a registered nurse, that it was too late. "They've killed him!" she wailed, falling to her knees at his side. "They've killed him! They've killed my husband!"

It was 3:15 in the afternoon when Malcolm's blood-covered body was brought on a stretcher into Columbia Presbyterian's emergency room. A team of doctors performed an on-the-spot tracheotomy in an attempt to help him breathe, then slit open his chest in order to massage his heart, only to find that bullets had torn most of it away and had riddled both lungs and the aorta. After several minutes the doctors stitched Malcolm back up and covered him with a sheet. A short while later, a hospital spokesman entered the crowded office where Betty and a group of Malcolm's friends were waiting and announced that "the gentleman you knew as Malcolm X" was dead.

During the week that followed, thousands of people, black and white, braved bomb threats and freezing weather to pay their last respects to Malcolm. A single floral piece adorning the outsized coffin in which he lay in his familiar minister's garb was inscribed, "To El-Hajj Malik, from Betty." Before he was laid to rest the next Saturday, the following events occurred: Harlem's Muslim Mosque Number 7 was burned down by "parties unknown"; the police apprehended three black men, two of them Black Muslims, and charged them with Malcolm's murder (although all three were later found guilty, the prosecution was never able to establish just who had ordered the killing); and in Chicago, at the Nation of Islam's "Savior's Day" Convention that very Friday, when the Honorable Elijah Muhammad rose to speak, his fez-topped head was barely visible above a wall of grim-faced Muslim bodyguards. "For a long time Malcolm stood here where I stand," the Messenger declared in an emotional speech during which he frequently lapsed into fits of coughing. "In those days, Malcolm was safe, Malcolm was loved. God Himself protected Malcolm. . . . He was a star who went astray! Who was he leading? Who was he teaching? . . . I lifted him up and he came back preaching that we should not take the enemy as an enemy. . . . They know I didn't harm Malcolm. They know I loved him. His foolish teachings brought him to his own end!"

On Saturday, February 27, 1965, Malcolm was buried at the Ferncliff Cemetery in Ardsley, New York, to the accompaniment of Muslim prayers, his head turned to the east in accordance with Islamic tradition. ("All this," a black American government official scoffed earlier in the week, "about an ex-convict, ex-dope peddler who became a racial fanatic.") The day after the funeral a story about Malcolm in *The New York Times* explained how on the Last Day of Judgment, according to the Koran, "the graves open and men are called to account by Allah. The blessed, the Godfearing, the humble, the charitable, are summoned to the Garden of Paradise. There, according to the teaching of Muhammad, the Prophet, they live forever by flowing streams, reclining on silken cushions, and enjoying the company of dark-eyed maidens and wives of perfect purity."

In Harlem, a hand-printed placard in a bookstore window provided Malcolm with its own epitaph:

> Man, if you think Bro. Malcolm is dead
> You are out of your cotton-picking head,
> Just get up off your slumbering bed,
> And watch his fighting spirit spread.
> Every shut eye ain't sleep,
> Every goodbye ain't gone.

And out on Long Island, where Betty and the children were being put up by friends, six-year-old Attilah wrote a letter to her father. "Dear Daddy," it read, "I love you so. O dear, O dear, I wish you wasn't dead."

SOURCES

A great deal has been written about, as well as by, the renowned protagonists of this book, and in the course of my research I tried to avail myself of as wide a variety of this material as possible. For more than a year I haunted New York's Forty-second Street Library, immersing myself in obituaries, newspaper accounts, magazine articles, and what seemed an endless number of biographies (a complete bibliography of these alone would total close to one hundred titles). Listed below are books that I found especially helpful and which I recommend as a starting point for readers eager to learn more about the deaths and lives recounted in these pages.

Sigmund Freud

Jones, Ernest. *The Life and Work of Sigmund Freud.* New York: Basic Books, 1961.

Schur, Max. *Living and Dying.* New York: International Universities Press, 1972.

Harry Houdini

Gibson, Walter, and Young, Morris. *Houdini on Magic.* New York: Dover Publications, 1953.

Gresham, William Lindsay. *Houdini.* New York: Holt, Rinehart & Winston, 1959.

Houdini, Harry. *A Magician Among the Spirits.* New York: Harper Brothers, 1924.

Kellock, Harold. *Houdini, His Life Story: From the Recollections and Documents of Beatrice Houdini.* New York: Harcourt Brace, 1928.

Sources

Robert Falcon Scott

Huxley, Elspeth. *Scott of the Antarctic.* New York: Atheneum, 1978.

Ludlum, Harry. *Captain Scott: The Full Story.* London: Foulsham, 1965.

Pound, Reginald. *Scott of the Antarctic.* London: Cassell, 1966.

Scott, Robert Falcon. *The Voyage of the Discovery.* London: Smith, Elder, 1905.

Scott, Robert Falcon. *Scott's Last Expedition.* London: J. Murray, 1968.

Isadora Duncan

Duncan, Isadora. *My Life.* New York: Liveright, 1927.

Macdougall, Allan Ross. *A Revolutionary in Art and Love.* New York: Thomas Nelson, 1960.

Seroff, Victor. *The Real Isadora.* New York: Dial Press, 1971.

Terry, Walter. *Isadora Duncan: her life, her art, her legacy.* New York: Dodd Mead, 1964.

Benito Mussolini

Collier, Richard. *Duce!* New York: Viking Press, 1971.

Fermi, Laura. *Mussolini.* Chicago: University of Chicago Press, 1963.

Kirkpatrick, Sir Ivone. *Mussolini; A Study in Power.* New York: Hawthorn Books, 1964.

Whittle, Peter. *One Afternoon at Mezzegra.* Englewood Cliffs, N.J.: Prentice-Hall, 1969.

Zelda Fitzgerald

Fitzgerald, Zelda. *Save Me the Waltz.* New York: Charles Scribner's Sons, 1932.

Sources

Milford, Nancy. *Zelda.* New York: Harper & Row, 1970.

Mizener, Arthur. *The Far Side of Paradise.* New York: Charles Scribner's Sons, 1951.

James Forrestal

Forrestal, James. *The Forrestal Diaries.* Edited by Walter Mills, with the collaboration of E. S. Duffield. New York: Viking Press, 1951.

Rogow, Arnold A. *James Forrestal: A Study of Personality, Politics, and Policy.* New York: Macmillan, 1963.

Yukio Mishima

Mishima, Yukio. *Confessions of a Mask.* New York: New Directions, 1958.

Nathan, John. *Mishima.* Boston: Little, Brown, 1974.

Scott-Stokes, Henry. *The Life and Death of Yukio Mishima.* New York: Farrar, Straus & Giroux, 1974.

Dylan Thomas

Brinnin, John Malcolm. *Dylan Thomas in America.* Boston: Little, Brown, 1955.

Ferris, Paul. *Dylan Thomas.* New York: Dial Press, 1977.

FitzGibbon, Constantine. *The Life of Dylan Thomas.* Boston: Atlantic–Little, Brown, 1965.

Thomas, Caitlin. *Leftover Life to Kill.* New York: Putnam's, 1957.

Thomas, Dylan. *Collected Poems.* New York: New Directions, 1953.

Malcolm X

Clarke, John Henrik, ed. *Malcolm X: The Man and His Times*. New York: Macmillan, 1969.

Goldman, Peter. *The Death and Life of Malcolm X*. New York: Harper & Row, 1975.

Malcolm X. *The Autobiography of Malcolm X*. With the assistance of Alex Haley. New York: Grove Press, 1965.